Overcoming the Overwhelming

How to Turn Adversity into Success

Terry!
You have the power to overcome. Use it!

CMC
6/30/81

Overcoming the Overwhelming

How to Turn Adversity into Success

Charles M. King

Oakhill Press

Cleveland, Ohio

Copyright 1991, Charles M. King

All rights reserved. Reproduction or translation of any part of this work beyond that permitted by Section 107 or 108 of the 1976 United States Copyright Act without the permission of the copyright owner is unlawful. Quotes or excerpts are permitted or further information should be addressed to the Permissions Department, Oakhill Press.

10 9 8 7 6 5 4 3 2

Library of Congress Cataloging-in-Publication Data

King, Charles M., 1934 —
    Overcoming the Overwhelming: how to turn adversity into success/Charles M. King

ISBN 0-9619590-4-5
1.   Success — Psychological aspects. 2. Success — Religious aspects-Christianity. I. Title.

ISBN 0-9619590-4-5

BF637, S8K486	1991		
158'.1 — dc20		90-19603	CIP

Oakhill Press books are available at special discounts for bulk purchases for sales promotions, premiums, fund-raising, or educational use. For details, contact the publisher.

Oakhill Press
7449 Oakhill Road
Cleveland, Ohio 44146-5901
(216) 646-9999

Printed in the United States of America

Dedication

With deep gratitude and respect, I dedicate this book to Jessie, my dear wife of thirty-four years. She was my inspiration and encouragement to be an overcomer. Somehow I believe she is rejoicing from heaven over its publication.

About the Author

Charles Murray King grew up in segregated, rural Columbia, South Carolina. During his formative years, people of his race were deprived of full citizenship privileges. In this environment he learned how to excel and be an achiever. King took the lessons learned in this tough environment and assimilated them into a tough-minded overcoming lifestyle. He mastered the art believing in himself and his creative mind to become a consistent overcomer.

Following his undergraduate study at A&T State University in Greensboro, North Carolina, King embarked on an illustrious career as an officer in the United States Army in the area of guided missiles. Though he majored in Economics and Sociology, King mastered the complex missile technology and proceeded to become one of the most celebrated guided missile instructors ever to teach at the Army's prestigious Guided missile School at Fort Bliss, Texas. Later in his military career, King became commanding officer of one of the Army's most complex missile systems, the Pershing I.

After eleven years of "Continuously Outstanding" service, King obtained a Masters Degree from Kent State University. He began his civilian career as a very productive salesman.

In 1972, King founded his own consulting and training firm, Goald Incorporated. Many advised him not to start such a venture, because corporations were not likely to employ his services to train and consult with the predominantly white management staffs that existed at that time. Disregarding this advice, King proceeded to become one of America's most moving and dynamic speakers and trainers in personal development, management and sales.

Goald has provided services to such blue chip companies as Allen Bradley, Babcock and Wilcox, Central States Can Company, Firestone Tire and Rubber, General Electric, The Former Goodyear Aerospace, Hygienic Corporation, Ohio Bell, Ohio Edison and many others.

Having rebounded from terminal illness and numerous other personal and business adversities, Charles King has developed a tenacious and sure outlook that is obvious in the personal confidence and faith that characterize his seminars, speeches, and consulting.

Charles King is believable and genuinely inspirational because he's been there! Even in the face of terminal illness, King took charge of the medical staff administering to him and led them to success in combating his malady.

King's same confidence comes through with equal power in this very relevant book.

For more than twenty years Charles King has been electrifying audiences, arming them with information and skills that can be used in personal and professional lives.

Listed in Who's who in the Midwest since 1982, King is frequently referred to by his clients as an extremely effective consultant as well as "friend and confidant".

From his base in Anderson, Indiana, Charles King travels nationally spreading his dynamic message of human possibility. To schedule him to work with your organization, contact him at 1104 Indian Mound Drive, Anderson, Indiana 46013; (317) 649-5389.

Overcoming the Overwhelming

Table of Contents

1. Imagination — Seeing Your Victory First 9
2. Purposing — Staying on Top of Circumstances 32
3. The Self Image of an Overcomer 42
4. The Plan — Something to Imagine 65
5. Desire — The Motivator 78
6. Idea Generation — An Endless Process 90
7. Pray Without Ceasing 100
8. Yea Though I Walk 115

Preface

Charles M. King has spent most of his life trying to motivate others.

His keen insight, wisdom and plain ol' common sense have served as catalysts in helping others achieve their goals.

Although he has faced much adversity in his personal life, Charles applied his own beliefs, faith and principles to overcome these adversities.

While "No Man Is An Island, No Man Stands Alone," Charles fortifies this statement in this thought-provoking book.

In the following pages, Charles provides a formula for success and peace of mind. His common sense approach to creativity acknowledges that we all have the tools to "Overcome The Overwhelming."

A person of unending faith, endurance and hope, Charles paints a portrait of how to get the most out of life.

I have known Charles M. King for many years and this book is a testimony of his conviction.

You will benefit immensely from its contents.

Albert E. Fitzpatrick
Assistant Vice President/Minority Affairs
Knight-Ridder, Inc.
(A communications company)

Foreword

On March 6, 1988, the doctors told Charles King he only had six months to live...at the outside. He was a victim of renal cell carcinoma — cancer in the right kidney. There was little that medical science could do.

Charles knew there was more he could do! He decided to listen to his own "medicine" that he'd been sharing with others for years as a management consultant and inspirational speaker.

Result? Charles King is alive today. To the amazement of the doctors, in a year-long bout Charles conquered cancer using the philosophies and techniques he'll share in this book. What a triumph!

Charles has overcome a host of obstacles and setbacks in his life. Faced with his challenges, most of us would just give up. Too many of us give up when confronted by much less than what this man has beaten. He's applied his principles in some astounding ways!

In the following pages, you'll discover how an unabashed faith in God, combined with a powerful and exciting use of imagination, can make a profound difference in your life.

The pages of this book could be filled with stories about how Charles King's work changed the lives of those who have heard him. Instead, Charles has chosen to talk directly with you, from the heart. Prepare to enjoy a vivid, inspirational, and instructional conversation with someone who cares about you, even though you've never met. You'll feel his sincerity coming through.

With the repeated confirmations that his principles really do work, really do make a difference, it's highly appropriate that Charles King shares them with us.

Enjoy and grow.

Roger E. Herman, CSP
Author of The Process of
Excelling and Keeping
Good People

Introduction

The most prevalent vehicle for being a master of life is Imagination. In this book we are going to treat it as the pivotal element, given us by God to overcome whatever besets us in this life.

As we pursue this fascinating subject, I will ask you to agree with me on several points; the first of which is that we were designed to master life, regardless of the vicissitudes that come our way. We are not to be stymied, but to be creative masters, finding ways to address the next issue and the next. We will contend that whenever you become "whipped," it is a decision.

Even if you can't totally accept what I've said to this point, at least concede the possibility and read on. Because we won't be dealing in conjecture but actual cases and practical points that make sense. Somewhere along the way you'll want to believe it. After all, it is to our advantage to believe it.

"Anything the mind of man can conceive and believe, it can achieve." These are the words expressed boldly by Napoleon Hill in his success primer, *Think and Grow Rich*. This poignant phrase has been maligned, doubted, cursed and reduced to the lowest level of slang and folly. Nonetheless, it is true. A prerequisite, however, is that you believe. Let me say early, and this I promise: what you believe, you'll get.

In so many seminars I've had people try to stump me on this point by offering such responses as, "I can believe

I can fly all I want but that won't make me fly." My usual response is once you move beyond hypothesis to true belief, you'll find a way. After all, the Wright brothers did. Others say, "I can believe all I want but I won't be a professional athlete when I'm fifty." To this I say, "When you really do, you probably will." But the question I say is do we really know the difference between belief and hypothesis?

At one point in my life I might have said, "I can believe all I want, that I, as a black man, can ever go into some American corporation day after day and train and consult with sophisticated managers all I want but it'll never happen." Well let me say that when I truly believed it and desired it, my imagination gave me avenues by which I could make it happen. For the past twenty years it has happened; even to my amazement.

Hill said anything the mind can conceive. In this book I will contend that anything one can imagine and act on can be achieved. It must be understood, however, that true belief produces action in support of that belief. Although Hill and I agree in principle, I will be taking a somewhat different approach to get to the same place — success and an overcoming life.

I contend that we are so powerful in our imaginations that even the universe and all of its elements will reorient themselves in response to that which is vividly imagined. It is indeed fascinating to ponder this contention. I have been tracking it for over twenty years. I have seen it work in so many ways. I have walked through the valleys and shadows of death. I have been penniless. I have been overcome with despair and I have been in places where I seemed trapped for some, only to be lifted and set on safe ground by imagination and positive action.

Overcoming the Overwhelming

If you read with objectivity you are in for a life changing experience. No matter where you are, at the pinnacle or at the point of doom, an active imagination can lift you if you make some new decisions about life, yourself, and the powerful resources that were designed in each of us.

As you read this book you will come to realize that much of what we all call impossible is merely impractical. This impracticality can be overcome when we recognize that so many things that were once impractical are now happening as a matter of course. We humans keep reaching greater heights of civilization because someone chooses to make the impractical, practical.

As you read on you will probably be challenged and startled by some of the possibilities for your life which you will discover. You must realize by now, imagination will be the main focus of this work, so let's examine it now. Although the title of this book is Overcoming The Overwhelming, we spend much of it talking about staying on top of circumstances and creating a comfortable and peaceful life.

Overcoming means being on top of life. It means self control, it means mastering discouragement, it means being resilient and bouncing back quickly.

Being an overcomer also means being tough minded enough not to lose a lot of time with discouragement and disappointment. Finally it means knowing who you are, where you're going and how you'll get there. From experience I know all of this to be possible, even expected by God. To back up His expectation He gave us the equipment to master circumstances: imagination, a creative mind with problem-solving capacities.

Because He knew what was available to us, Jesus,

acting as a model, tells us: "In the world ye shall have tribulation: but be of good cheer; I have overcome the world." If we will follow this great model we can also experience His victory and His joy as we consistently overcome what, for many, has been called overwhelming.

Chapter 1

Imagination — Seeing Your Victory First

The Power of Imagination

Perhaps you have heard someone respond to a statement or concept of yours as being a figment of your imagination or "child's stuff," unreal or floating somewhere above the earth. The implication being that if it is imagined, it is unreal and has very little chance of being true or real.

Imagination can be the fertile breeding ground for reality. If you can fix a thought or concept in your imagination, hold it there and develop desire for the reality of it, you can be well on your way to being highly creative and effective. Your only limits will be the limits of your imagination.

Cities, factories, buildings, inventions, art and every other form of creation including wealth and, in many instances, even the new born baby started in someone's imagination. It seems that imagination is a process originated by God which He provided to each of us as an instrument of our personal creative process. We can use imagination as He did to create and bring forth that which is important to us.

Imagination is truly the place where you sincerely want the concept to begin germinating.

Far too many of us treat our imaginative powers as tools of folly, fantasy or self-deception. I have believed strongly in the imaginative process for years. In speeches, seminars, and on cassette tapes, I was able to state specific personal experiences where it worked. I am even more sure of its effectiveness now; because as I will show you, imagination has become an instrument of life and death significance to me.

Let us journey together all the way back to the time of God's creation of the world. At that point, as recorded in the book of Genesis in the Bible, we note that God Himself first described, by use of words, the mental image of what He was about to create. In every case, it took physical form.

"And God said let there be light...and God said let there be a firmament..." and in each case there became what He had said or visualized first. As a creation of God, and in His likeness, we have been designed to function in much the same manner as He functions.

For some reason, however, there is usually a span of time and considerable effort expended before the concepts of our imaginations are realized. They will become real only if we hold the picture and follow the ideas that flow to us as a result of that picture.

Isn't it wonderful to have the power of mentally picturing objects or conditions we desire? As these mental pictures become more vivid, they somehow affect our emotions. These emotions drive us to motivation and inspiration which are the forerunners of action. These

Overcoming the Overwhelming 11

actions seem to come upon us by impulse at times and by ideas, "hunches," or strong urges at others. As we perform the actions, we systematically convert the pictures in our imaginations into reality.

It is my view that the body's neural system does not know the difference between a real or imagined circumstance. A circumstance strongly imagined or a situation vividly perceived can produce joy, great peace, debilitating anger or a host of other personal conditions that, at the time they are happening, seem very real.

Have you ever been angered by something or someone you thought or imagined meant to be a certain way, only to discover later that what you imagined was not the case? Didn't your body produce real emotions and feelings on the basis of what you imagined to be true at the time?

Imagination is a fascinating phenomenon which can render one extremely creative and produce in his life, either negative or positive results.

It would be beneficial to summarize at this point:

1. We all imagine something.
2. In response to our strong imaginings, we perform the acts dictated by impulse, ideas, hunches or urges or any combination of these.
3. Persisting in the above produces a new reality, either positive or negative.
4. Imagination is our primary means of being creative. Our well-being depends on it.

Please stop reading for just a moment and reflect on these significant points.

As a matter of background to highlight the usefulness of imagination, I would like to relate another story recorded in the book of Genesis in the Bible. This is the story of the Biblical character, Jacob, the son of Isaac. Jacob, being in a far away land, had agreed to serve his new father-in-law, Labon, for a period of seven years in exchange for the hand of Labon's daughter, Rachael, in marriage.

Because of the craftiness and deception of Labon, Jacob was constrained to work for him for a second period of seven years. Even after the second seven years, after which Jacob had planned to return to the land of his family, Labon urged him to remain even another seven years.

Realizing that Labon was becoming extremely wealthy on his labor, Jacob confronted Labon about the situation. Labon made an agreement to pay him by assigning to him "all the speckled and spotted cattle and all the brown cattle among the sheep, and the spotted and speckled among the goats."

Following the agreement, Labon decided to remove all of the cattle of this type from the herd, thinking Jacob would have little chance of accumulating a significant number of the herd which he had agreed to assign to him. Understanding the principles of imagination, Jacob was not to be outdone. He devised a means of reproducing offsprings from the cattle which would insure that he obtained an abundance of the cattle which Labon agreed to assign to him. This plan was to make Jacob very wealthy.

The living translation of the Bible describes Jacob's ingenious plan as follows:

> "Then Jacob took fresh shoots from poplar, almond and plane trees, and peeled white streaks in them, and placed those rods besides the watering troughs so that the flocks would see them when they came to drink, for that is when they mated. So the flocks mated before the white streaked rods, and their offsprings were streaked and

Overcoming the Overwhelming 13

spotted, and Jacob added them to his flock. Then he divided out the ewes from Labon's flock and separated them from the rams and let them mate only with Jacob's black rams. Thus he built his flock from Labon's."

"Moreover, he watched for the stronger animals to mate, and placed the peeled branches before them, but didn't with the feeble ones. So the less healthy lambs were Labon's and the stronger ones were Jacob's!"

"As a result, Jacob's flock increased rapidly and he became very wealthy, with many servants, camels and donkeys."

This remarkable story points out the fact that Jacob, with great ingenuity, devised a means through the concept of imaging to reproduce cattle with spots, speckles and stripes. From somewhere, Jacob learned the principles of imagination and he used them successfully, even with the breeding of cattle.

For the purposes of our study, let's see if we can develop a workable definition for imagination. I'd like to pique your interests to the extent that you will want to explore imagination and find applications of it for your personal productivity and overall victorious living.

Imagination is a personal facility available to everyone. I believe it to be a Divine design feature whereby God empowers us to develop mental pictures to guide our actions. The use of imagination enables us to create what we vividly and tenaciously hold as a picture of our personal reality. In other words, if you can envision something and hold that vision, you are well on your way to seeing it realized, desired or not.

So, let's define imagination as the act or power of forming mental pictures of items, conditions, or attributes not yet present in reality. Further let's say that those vivid pictures become the blueprint for one's reality.

Imagination consists of the act or power of creating mental images of that which has never been experienced, or the creation of new conditions by combining experiences and usual conditions in new ways. Imagination might further be described as the forerunner of creation. I firmly believe that imagination is a force of creation that sets elements of the surroundings into motion and it brings them together no matter where they are, into the situation or condition imagined.

Although specific action and intense performance is vital to the process, I have come to know that certain other actions take place in response to our imaginings over which we exercise little or no control. It is at this point that many refer to these type actions as fate, luck, or "someone smiled on me." Most of us would concede that some things just happen to bring about final reality.

I have a great love for stories and accounts of people who have achieved wonderful things in their lives. I read biographies and autobiographies as often as I can. I'm amazed at the successes that have come to achievers when they least expected it or "never in my wildest imagination would I have thought it possible."

There are even times when accidents have proven to be timely events bringing the achiever just what he needed to complete the process with which he was struggling. Charles Goodyear is such an example. He was seeking a means of hardening rubber for tires when some of his compound spilled on to a hot stove. The resulting hardening of the compound led him to the vulcanizing process.

Although these people labored painstakingly, with great desire and determination, there have always been those events which took place to complement their efforts — events over which they had little or no control. The imaginative powers, coupled with faith, affect the elements of the universe and influence their movement into a configuration that responds favorably to the entity being vividly imagined.

Sarte writes: "We have seen that the act of imagination is a magical one. It is an incantation destined to produce the objects of one's thoughts, the things one desires, in the manner that one can take possession of it." While I would reject the notion of it being magical, I would suggest that the remainder of Sarte's statement is extremely accurate.

In place of magical, I prefer to say that imagination is a function of the power of God, ordained by Him and designed to rearrange the elements of the universe in response to the fervent wishes and aspirations of the individual. In a word, God placed man here and arranged the universe in such a way that it will respond to those who will use their imaginations in vivid ways.

What we state in the definition and in the subsequent discourse is the central theme of this book. It is my intention to make clear the process as I have seen it work so marvellously for me personally and as I have studied its influence on history.

The power of imagination is something I'd dare not discuss unless I had experienced it; not once or twice but numerous times. It is exceedingly unexciting as a discussion of theory or as a matter of speculation. As we proceed, I'll document aspects of this discussion with personal experiences as well as the experiences of others.

Because of the ever presence of the spirit power of God that lives in all of us, each and every one of us can truly know great possibilities and prosperity. The Spirit of God does not know, nor can it be known, in bondage. The Spirit that is committed to work in our behalf cannot be bound and, when we strive to work in harmony with Him, neither can we. Therefore, let us state unequivocally, that those who are overwhelmed are exercising the choice to be that way.

As spiritual humans, we possess unlimited possibility. Unfortunately, far too many focus too frequently on negative and limited possibilities. We imagine the negatives and the limits. We defend our negative thinking and eventually become comfortable living with negative conditions. We can easily convince ourselves that positive possibility is out of our reach except for a "lucky break" here and there, or if "God should happen to open up and drop something on us," solely by chance.

We often see the positive as something for someone else at another place at another time. All too often people who have experienced a few disappointing events in their lives become enamored with negative feelings and actions which rule their condition. Even with the tools of success at their disposal, they do not achieve because disappointments have created debilitating negative attitudes and feelings.

I challenge each reader to take charge of the rich resource that God has designed into him or her. See and focus on the positive possibilities. Take back your mind and allow the Spirit to restore your vision of that which has always been possible to everyone.

Using God's character we can create a life, a business, a family or any other circumstance, filled with positive possibility and opportunity. As I share these principles with you, I feel very authoritative. In order to accomplish things in my life, I've had to put countless negative experiences into proper perspective.

My experience has taught me that there are three forms of imagination. Each has utility for certain efforts and aspects of our lives, depending on the aspirations we have.

Idealized Image

The first is the idealized-image. This is an expanded estimation and awareness of one's self, derived from lofty thoughts about one's self. This comes from thinking about what we would prefer to be, rather than what we actually are. The exercise of this concept of imagination is discussed in the chapter on Self Image.

George Washington Carver held rigidly to this concept of imagination as he lived his life. Born to slave parents in 1864 in Missouri, Carver was left fatherless in his infancy. Stolen and carried into Arkansas, he was purchased from his captors for a race horse worth $300.00. After being returned to his home in Missouri, Carver worked his way through high school in Minneapolis, Kansas. This in itself was quite a feat for a person just out of slavery; in fact, it was almost unheard of. To add additional wonder, Carver later obtained a degree from Iowa State College of Agriculture and Mechanic Arts.

Later Carver conducted experiments in soil management and crop production. In Alabama, where blacks were not very highly regarded, he urged planters to raise peanut and sweet potato crops to replenish the nutrients in the soil depleted by cotton crops.

Carver worked extensively with the peanut and produced hundreds of by-products, including milk and coffee substitutes along with numerous other well-known products including soap, flour, ink, and even shaving cream. When the menacing boll weevil nearly ruined cotton crops, Carver came to the rescue and demonstrated ways to turn to alternate crops such as peanuts and sweet potatoes.

Carver's work enabled southern farmers, white and black alike, to continue earning an income. The land, which had been exhausted by cotton, was renewed and the south became a significant supplier of new agricultural products. All of this may be attributed to the ingenuity of a person once sold for a mere $300.00. He evidently had a much higher estimation of his own worth in his imagination.

Carver became the first scientist to create synthetic marble from wood shavings. During World War II, he conducted experiments which led to the replacement of textile dyes which had been formerly imported from Europe. All together he produced dyes of some 500 shades.

In 1953, in recognition of his remarkable contributions, Carver's birthplace was made into a national monument. It is marked by a plaque and bronze bust. It is a monument built to a man who was born to slaves and who became an educator, researcher, scientist, and a benefactor to his fellow man and to his country. This is truly remarkable for one whose actual status was that of mere chattel. Somehow, however, Carver looked beyond the overwhelming social image and visualized his ideal self. Apparently he did it with such conviction that he experienced the joy of living this ideal image. Once on this course, the actual is never again the ultimate. Carver's ideal image kept him increasingly more productive. That's the way the process works.

Obviously Carver had numerous reasons to be negative about himself and life around him; he also had reason enough to be a doubter, but there must have been that more attractive positive flicker of light and hope that kept his ideal image alive.

Creative Imagination

The second type of imagination is the creative imagination. It is self-initiated and self-organized. This type of imagination is the beginning point of invention in that it

Overcoming the Overwhelming

leads to the design of something useful. Because of its value to all of us in solving problems, creating new inventions, and rising above circumstances, we will focus on this type extensively.

No doubt everyone can think of at least one person who fits this category. There are numerous fascinating and remarkable accounts of people just like you and me who excelled and made contributions to the well-being of millions through their effective use of the inventive aspects of imagination. There is Ben Franklin and his advancement in and practical use of electricity. There is Dr. Charles Drew and his amazing work in developing blood plasma. There is Madame C. J. Walker and her beauty and treatment products for black females. How about Alexander Graham Bell and the telephone?

Consider Charles Spaulding, a black man who built a successful insurance company against great odds. Let's include Burroughs and the adding machine. We could continue naming people who used this form of imagination successfully — all the way to Walter Hunt who, in just a few minutes, used his imagination to give us a nifty device called the safety pin as for back as 1825.

One of the fascinating examples is that of Chester Carlson who, after his graduation from the California Institute of Technology in 1930, became an employee in the patent department of a New York electronics firm. During his early days in the job he observed a constant demand for multiple copies of patent specifications. Noting the shortcomings of carbon copies and the fact that only a few could be made at a time, many of which were blurred, Carlson began toying with the idea of other means of making copies.

Soon after recognizing the need and visualizing various means of meeting it, Carlson developed the idea of photoelectric effects as the key to a dry copying process involving no chemicals. Ideas followed...as is usually the case in creative imagination. As Carlson pursued each of the ideas, he eventually developed the xerography process, a derivative of the Greek word for "dry."

In 1948, after making agreements with the Batelle Memorial Institute and the Haloid Company, the first demonstration of the xerography process was conducted. Eleven years later the Haloid-Xerox Company, later to become the Xerox Corporation, introduced the first commercial dry copying machine.

This type of creativity over the centuries has made life much easier and productive for all of us. It begins when an individual such as Carlson dare to use creative imagination. Usually there is a strong conviction that the possibility exists and the individual desires to see it actualized.

Anticipatory Imagination

The final classification is that of anticipatory imagination. This form represents movement toward a specific goal, sufficiently specific to be clearly visualized and held in the imagination. Again, there are numerous examples of individuals who have used this form of imagination to a remarkably successful degree. One of my favorite examples is the meteoric rise of Darwin Davis.

Blocked by racial discrimination when he graduated from college in Arkansas, Davis was unable to gain access to the opportunities offered to some citizens by corporate America. Although he had an obsessing desire to be a salesman, the lack of opportunity for blacks sidetracked him. Instead, Davis became a mathematics teacher in the public school system of Detroit.

Davis never abandoned his desire to become a sales-

Overcoming the Overwhelming 21

man and eventually a corporate officer. Gradually, as the corporate doors began to open for Black Americans, Davis found and pursued an opportunity to become a salesman for Equitable Life Insurance Company. Even after ten successful years as a teacher, his goal of having a corporate career was still intact.

In 1967, Davis's first year as a sales agent, he earned membership in the Million Dollar Roundtable, the prestigious organization of people who write a million dollars or more in insurance in one year. By 1975 Davis had advanced to the position of Agency Vice President. The track he was running on made him one of the fastest climbers in Equitable's history. He has received every management honor that the company gives.

In 1976, just nine years after he joined Equitable, Davis led his department to generate $840 million in sales! Today he is a senior Vice President of the company and, as such, is among a select few Black Americans in line to head a major American corporation.

Finally, given an opportunity to pursue his goal, Davis was like a "cocked pistol" ready to be fired. His is a classic case of anticipatory imagination. Although his circumstances made his anticipated achievement seem unlikely, once the opportunity appeared he seized that which had been firmly etched in his mind. It is likely, however, that he never imagined the rapid rise in the corporation which he experienced. His goal was to be a successful salesperson, which by his words, is "the most powerful of all professions in the world." He never lost the vision or image.

I invite you to stop at this point and examine your circumstances. Can you cite personal experiences relating to each of the three classes of imagination?

A) *The idealized image is an expanded estimation of your self based on what you would like to be rather than the actual person in the circumstances existing around you. Perhaps you have abandoned the idealized image because you felt it was unrealistic or because you felt it was too immodest to think that way. One or more of these factors could have caused you to feel uncomfortably guilty or foolish.*

If you address these concerns, you should be prepared to confront and overcome the discouragements that will come from deep in your own mind as well as from the words and gestures of those around you. You must believe strongly enough to go it alone, if you must. Later we will introduce some action steps to assist you in strengthening your idealized image. For now I urge you to control and abandon the negative thoughts that can surface and mar your progress.

B) *Creative imagination is a self initiated organized imagination which is the beginning point of invention leading to the design of something useful. Most of us have thought of at least one thing which would solve problems, overcome obstacles or make life easier for ourselves or others. Most of us negate the thought by saying, "If it was a such a great idea, some smart person would have done it already."*

Many think that all inventions were the brain-child of some genius or brilliant engineer, well educated and well trained. Seldom do we stop to think that most of the minds that created so many of the concepts and useful innovations we enjoy could not gain employment at some of the companies that have developed as a result of their inventions.

Overcoming the Overwhelming

Henry Ford was a sixth-grade dropout. Thomas Edison, who gave us so many useful inventions, attended school for a total of three months. I don't think Ben Franklin went beyond the second grade in school. Frederick Douglas, the Black American orator, statesman and publisher was an escaped slave who never entered any school until he entered to deliver a speech. Benjamin Banneker, a Black astronomer and architect instrumental in the engineering, surveying, and subsequent layout of the city of Washington, D. C. was completely self-taught. If you have discovered a certain inventiveness about yourself, perhaps you should pursue it; you may have the answer to something very significant.

Consider some of the following characteristics which have been found to be important to those who have a strong desire to pursue their creative urges or become overcomers. If you have a number of these perhaps you should consider persevering. If you don't have them, perhaps you can develop them:

- independent thought and action
- tenacity
- courage
- the ability to develop strong convictions
- persistence
- discipline
- curiosity and inquisitiveness
- resilience
- resourcefulness
- stick-to-itiveness

In this aspect of creativeness, we are either creating something that never existed or bringing old elements together to work in different ways. This aspect is good for organizations as well as for individuals. In fact, organizations of the future must turn heavily to this kind of imagination and encourage it in their employees if they expect to remain healthy and resourceful. The requirement will be great as we enter the fierce competition of the global market place. It will be the brainstorming of multi-faceted corporate teams that will keep companies on the leading edge in their markets.

> C) *Anticipatory imagination: This is goal-setting which will be discussed fully in our planning segment. Think of something you truly desire to accomplish, be it ever so small, and break it into four or fewer major components. Maybe it's just to save for the down payment on a home or new car, to purchase new furniture or a suit or dress. Perhaps it's just the desire to be a better person by developing certain new attributes.*

Any one of these can be visualized, so I urge you to start practicing the visualization of something you truly desire. Break it into manageable segments and determine what you can do immediately to work toward achievement of the first segment. Don't stop visualizing until it is yours. Note the enthusiasm and confidence it builds.

Consider this review very carefully before moving on. Imagination could be one of the most important undertakings of your life, young or old, regardless of your current status or condition.

Using Imagination in Your Life

After much study and reflection, I have taken the time to develop a recommended process for living above circumstances and being an overcomer. Because these principles have meant so much to my life, I want to share them.

Overcoming the Overwhelming 25

I am absolutely certain they can be as helpful to you as they've been to me. Bear in mind also that these principles were not organized when I used them. By using them they should enable you to soar even higher, quicker, if you choose.

Imagination will bring to your awareness the great benefits God has in store for those who correctly use the creative resource He has provided. It is the key to inventiveness, creation, prosperity and positive self-development or group development.

In the past several years process names have been ascribed to imagination such as the process name of Imagineering used by The Disney Company. Apparently such names were chosen because they suggest a relationship to such disciplines as mechanical, structural or architectural engineering. These are all considered acts of maneuvering or managing machines, structures, and buildings to form new realities.

The mechanical engineer designs machines and, working with the machinist, determines new processes and elements which the machine can perform and produce. The architect and the structural engineer perform similar tasks on structures and buildings in harmony with builders.

In like manner, process names such as Imagineering suggest using creative devices such as one's own personality, attitude and imagination and the several creative devices of others to form new realities. In this sense imagination is a kind of engineering, the kind that God ordained to lift each of us to great heights as we use our talents.

These process names might be new terms to you, but, in all likelihood, imagination is not. By use of this concept, these originators seek to bring all of the facilities and resources of the imagination into clear focus for daily practical use.

Imagination, of course, is not new, for there have been daily uses of it since God created the earth. When asked how he came to discover the Laws of Gravity, Newton replied, "I thought about it all the time." He held it in his imagination until the ideation was induced. Following ideation came the realization and the development of the specific laws.

A great sculptor of marble elephants, when asked how he performed his work with such detail, replied. "I see the elephant in the stone before I begin..." Imagination, what fascination, what possibility? In the constructive use of this power, the conscious mind functions in harmony with the mind of God which only knows possibilities. It is through this harmony that man's "wildest imagination" can be actualized.

Were it not for the development of this process in 1984, and my use of it in so many ways in ensuing years I probably would not be alive today. As it has meant much to others, it has meant life to me. Before I give the details of the life and death situation, however, I want to tell you how I came to develop this sure fire process in the first place.

In the summer of 1982 my eldest son graduated from the University. In addition to receiving a degree in Business Management, he was commissioned a Second Lieutenant in the U. S. Air Force with orders to attend flight training at one of the Air Force's Flight Training Centers.

He had worked very hard to get a "flying slot" with the Air Force. After much adversity and difficulty during his college years, he had finally reached a significant milestone. He was close to fulfillment of his childhood dream of being a pilot.

Overcoming the Overwhelming

In achieving his goal, he had to cling tenaciously to his dream and the vision of the future. There were many days during those college years that, for various reasons, it looked bleak. But now victory had finally come and he had earned the right to attend flight school. The reality of a dream come true was just ten months away.

In the early days of his flight training, my son sent home glowing reports of his progress in the school. To say the least, we were very proud of him. Having watched him struggle for five years, and now to hear the good reports, it seemed like victory was close at hand.

One evening, however, he called to inform us that he had run into difficulty in trying to execute a certain maneuver in his trainer aircraft. He said they were going to give him another try at it, but if he failed the next attempt, things didn't look good for his remaining in the program.

There was a strong possibility he would "wash out" of flight training. Noting the sound of discouragement in his voice, I urged him to seize the next opportunity and give it his best. He said he would and, after a small chat, we hung up the phone.

Because I believe prayer can change things, as you will see later, I took time out daily to pray for his success. In addition, I visualized him executing that maneuver over and over. On his next call, however, the news was not good. He had once again failed the maneuver and had already been dismissed from flight training.

Because of his academic standing in the class, he was being allowed to remain in the Air Force. In a few weeks he would be transferred to another Air Force school for the purpose of receiving navigator's training.

I sensed his disappointment. Anyone who has ever

come to an apparent end to a lifelong dream can relate to his feelings as well.

My first inclination was to console him, accept the verdict and say, "Well, all is not lost; at least they're keeping you around." As I was shaping my mouth to utter these dismal words, I was stunned when I heard myself say, "No, we won't accept it. You went there to be a pilot and that's what you'll be!" We were both shocked at what we heard me say.

Being somewhat confused and perplexed, my son asked, "How will I do that? When the Air Force makes a decision it is final," he said. They don't just reverse their decisions." Though my words seemed ridiculous, even to me, I held tightly to them as I said, "We'll think of something."

At the moment, I felt as though I was "bluffing" or trying to con him because I knew of no possible recourse. But, even as I spoke, I became more and more convinced. After tiring of trying to talk some sense into me, he reluctantly went along with me.

As we hung up the phone, we agreed to continue visualizing him flying as an Air Force pilot, and not a navigator. Even though I felt helpless, I continued to hold the picture. I could do little else. He was on the hot seat and I was clinging to a seemingly ridiculous decree.

In my imagination, and hopefully my son's, I was taking on the steel trap decision of the U. S. Air Force, attempting to reverse it. I had no contacts, no political attachments, nor any other "strings" that could be pulled. But the decision remained in my mind: "We will not accept it!"

Knowing how badly my son wanted to be a pilot, I knew he would be in my corner, hoping I could do something to make my imaginary decree a reality. Even

Overcoming the Overwhelming

though he had said to me: "There is nothing we can do to make the Air Force reverse its decision."

We waited it out as we prayed and visualized success... getting beyond the decision and success as a pilot. While waiting, my son discovered that sometimes, in a few cases, based on special circumstances, it was possible to appeal a ruling. When he informed us of this, we urged him to pursue it. "No matter how remote, go for it," I said.

My son proceeded with the appeal, discovering that he did, indeed, have grounds. His wing commander heard his case and consented to give him another chance. He was set back two classes and allowed to complete his flight training.

As I sat at the graduation ceremonies watching my son receive his wings and being assigned to fly B-52 aircraft for the Air Force, I could barely contain myself. At that moment I was thoroughly convinced of the power of imagination and the faithful response of God to it.

It became clear to me that imagination and visualization is what we have been given to make our dreams real and achieve our success. It was all we had and it was enough. I began to reflect on my personal achievements and discovered most of them had come by this means.

Each time I see my son take off or land in his large complex aircraft, I am reassured that through imagination and determination, no matter what the odds may be, we have command of the circumstances in our lives. To see him take off and land is a constant reminder of how realities develop. In my view, he has learned it also. Today he is an Air Force Captain and an instructor pilot on the B-52. For several years he was an Aircraft Commander. Soon he will leave the Air Force to become a commercial airline pilot.

Although there have been numerous other occasions

where this process works, it was this experience that inspired me first to share this concept through seminars, speeches, and audio cassette tapes a few years ago. The validation I have received from people who heard my message inspired me to write this book to share this concept with you.

Neither difficulties nor obstacles are sufficient reasons to abandon a dream. Even though you might feel burdened by the circumstances and vicissitudes of your life, the power to imagine is not defeated and will work as well as ever. Hold the image and follow the steps outlined in this book, and your circumstances will eventually change to conform to that image.

With that background, let us proceed to discover the exciting principles in this book. As we do, I want to stress that this is not a new twist or wave to the positive thinking craze which reached fad proportions in the 1960's. During that era, some people came to capture the spirit of positive thinking as taught by Dr. Norman Vincent Peale, Napoleon Hill, Maxwell Maltz, and others. Many people literally changed their lives remarkably.

Others, however, thought they had found a something-for-nothing panacea. Such people moved about proclaiming all manner of problems solved through wishful thinking. Sick people denied their illness. Impoverished denied their poverty. Many used empty words, easily spoken, as something quite easy to do. Such a wave of expectations frustrate some and disillusion others.

In this book, I invite you to examine with me some principles and laws in a substantive and sober fashion.

First, realize that we must do more than verbalize the law; we must prove it. Newton proclaimed the law, but he held tenaciously to it until he proved it. Shakespeare wrote and kept his vision, expecting to receive the proper lines and characters. Mozart and Tchaikovsky proclaimed the law, but held the vision and worked and worked until the right notes came to complete their works.

As you study these principles, you should not only proclaim them, but let the great mind of God dictate right actions as you seek to make your imaginings a reality.

This approach to goal achievement is presented in individual segments around the principles we feel are necessary for success. We will discuss the following principles as the main ones for overcoming and remaining an overcomer:

- dynamic purpose
- self-image
- planning
- desire
- idea generation
- prayer and meditation

Chapter 2

Purposing —
Staying On Top of Circumstances

The first principle in the process is that of defining a purpose. It is extremely valuable to individual or organization effort. Let us refer to this as a formal step.

Purposing can be used for long-term life changes, as well as realization of short-term objectives. It can simply be used to achieve a singular goal or develop some personal attribute. It can be used in simple and informal ways, but we offer it with the hopes that each individual really will use it completely in managing his full life and in an ongoing fashion to reach great heights of achievement. It is even important to purpose to become an overcomer.

There is an abiding reason for the existence of every living creature. Nothing or no one is without purpose. As you observe and explore your surroundings, you will find that plants, animals and other creatures are fulfilling a divine purpose. They were created to perform some useful function and, if they could choose not to perform it, some aspect of the universal order would go lacking. The plants

Overcoming the Overwhelming 33

and lower animals perform their purposes instinctively; unlike humans, they have little or no choice.

Perhaps you've noticed that when certain species of animals are virtually extinct, people who pay close attention to their functions become alarmed because they know something of great importance to universal order is about to be neglected.

Humans can, out of lack of awareness or just plain rejection, choose not to fulfill their purposes. There are a number of tasks that most of us can perform well. Because of this versatility and with an overriding desire to earn a living, most of us stop short of defining and fulfilling our purpose. Most of us will never move beyond the quest for survival or meeting physical needs.

Others discover within themselves an ability to earn money and proceed to pursue that course. They follow money in spite of that "little something" that continues to gnaw at them, reminding them that something is missing. Those who pursue only monetary objectives fall short of personal fulfillment. A very small percentage reach that blissful and peaceful condition of life that accompanies the fulfillment derived from pursuing a purpose.

It is important to mention that most people who discover their purpose and pursue it, find that purpose by accident. They usually pursue it at considerable risk and possible general lack of acceptance until those around them comprehended it.

Often the establishment of purpose causes us to disregard the norm. Those who "march to a different drummer" are very committed to their objectives. Their disregard of what others may think of them strengthens their resolve to create their own parade.

In our discussion you will see that the establishment

of a life-long purpose will become a formalized process for you. Through this chapter, we'll assist you in deciding whether you want to go all out for a full and adventuresome life. Designing and committing to a purpose is the best known way to achieve this. After you've studied this chapter, I am certain you'll be more curious about why you're here. Of all the things you do well, I'm sure you'll be curious about what you can do best, what God has assigned to you.

Have you ever wondered why you are here or what you can do best? Have you really examined yourself to determine the things you do best, to explore and obtain a reasonable estimation of the range of your talents? Or perhaps you have asked yourself, " Where can I best serve?" How about "Am I doing all I'm capable of doing?" If you have asked these or similar questions, chances are you've received answers. If they did not concur with your lifestyle, or if they didn't appear reasonable or practical, you abandoned them. Those answers might have given you an opportunity for fulfillment and tremendous peace of mind.

If you can identify with these or similar circumstances, don't feel badly; it happens to a significant majority of us. These and similar questions lead us to discover our purpose or reason for being. Whether you pursue it or abandon it, Purpose is your ticket to mastering the life you've been given. Finding what you can do and setting out to do it will bring you a joy beyond anything you ever imagined.

This aspect of the process will introduce you to a self significantly greater than you perhaps imagined. As you reflect on your being—your talents and personal traits, here's hoping you'll take charge. Dedicate yourself to far exceed what you ever expected of yourself, regardless of

Overcoming the Overwhelming 35

age or personal condition. Just bear in mind that it is all up to you.

At this point, ask yourself:

1. What do I really need to be doing?
2. On what things do I want to bring all of the power of creation to bear?

- My complete life?
- My skills abilities and talents?
- A specific skill, ability or talent?
- The work I desire to do?
- My current position?
- A desired position?
- My entire career?
- My relationships?
- My family as a whole?
- Some family member?

A group or an organization might pose similar questions regarding:

- the health of the organization itself
- interpersonal relations in the organization
- future direction of the organization
- stability...is it strong enough to meet the challenges of future years?
- competitive activity
- our company's rank in our industry
- the profit projection
- identification of markets
- how well we're serving our markets
- how we can achieve additional sales, services
- how we rank with respect to skilled personnel
- are our plans complete?

- are we maximizing opportunities regarding:
- new products, new markets

Dredge up anything and everything that needs examining, bring it into focus, and take some time to assess it honestly. Make those and similar points the center of attention. Remember, don't rush it, take all the time you need.

If you are working with a group, ask each member to think over the key questions, then bring them together to hear and discuss their responses. Take notes and carefully review them.

Go slowly at this juncture and do not advance until you've decided what you will do about purpose. As you focus, I urge you to avoid considering personal constraints, inhibitions or limitations. Simply try, as much as you can, to allow your mind to expand as you reflect on these significant questions.

This process may require several attempts. Take as much time as you need, because, as you will see later, these questions are very important and have life-changing implications.

The statement of personal or group purpose you derive should be direct, clear, simple, motivating and, above all, desirable. If you find it difficult to relate to your resulting statement of purpose, don't be weary; simply hold on to it in your thoughts, even if you feel unrealistic or childish.

You may have developed a full purpose for your life already. If it seems odd or out of focus, it may be because you've prided yourself in being "practical" and "realistic," and the purpose statement may not fit these parameters. Eventually, it may be necessary to reexamine the boundaries of your realism and rationality stretching them as you feel comfortable.

Overcoming the Overwhelming

That's part of the technique of having a purpose statement as your first step. I'm sure it must have sounded a bit preposterous for the people around Andrew Carnegie, an uneducated and broke immigrant from Scotland, to hear him recite his lofty vision of improving the lot of mankind. Most would refer to this as an unrealistic purpose for a man in Carnegie's condition. What could a person with such humble means do to improve mankind? He could barely help himself.

For years, Carnegie worked menial jobs. In fact, he worked the railroad for twelve years as a laborer. Yet he never lost his vision of mankind being improved through his efforts. Keeping the image alive, Carnegie led the way in developing the steel industry into one of America's greatest and expansive enterprises. When the opportunity arose, he seized it and continued to pursue his purpose, holding it in his imagination. Because Carnegie did this, millions have benefitted through the years. Did he work hard? Yes, very hard and long.

In later years Carnegie, in order to amass the capital he needed, sold his interests to financier and industrialist, J. P. Morgan for over six hundred million dollars. He used most of the proceeds to continue to "improve mankind." As a result of his philanthropy, there are numerous Carnegie Libraries across America which are still supported by his endowments. He also donated organ consoles numbering in the thousands to churches. Carnegie was a small man with a large purpose, and with the tenacity to make his image a reality.

Alexander Graham Bell consistently held images of phone wires extending across America with people in one part of the country talking with people in other parts. Being an inventor and not a marketer or businessman, Bell met just the person he needed to help him actualize his long held image. He met Theodore Vail who, in 1878 took over the company and together they developed policies that shaped American Telephone and Telegraph into what it has become. Bell believed Vail was sent along in response to the image he held of forming an organization to "extend wires across the country."

Earlier, I suggested that intense emotions tend to stir the mind into fast action. Think of a time when you experienced strong feelings, such as anger. Remember how it stimulated your consciousness and practically took charge of your body, causing it to move and produce other emotional and physical responses to anger? As we will see in the chapter on desire, in order to build ourselves up to such intensity, we need a similar positive emotion. Desire is the greatest emotion known that fulfills this need.

The union of the conscious mind and the mind of God is at its strongest and most vivid point when stimulated by desire. This union isn't complete until there is a sharp image of an object or condition which is the focus of desire.

Take a moment and review this chapter, conduct the review I recommended earlier. See if there isn't something that comes to mind that piques an emotion of desire.

In summarizing Purpose, we must recognize clearly that we can live a full, productive life if we will take the time to explore and discover ourselves. Identify as accurately as you can that which you really want to do. If you have not discovered that yet, this is the book for you.

Soren Kierkegard once said, "Nothing can make a person sick sooner than feeling useless, unwanted, unchallenged and unneeded, or feeling that the values other men pursue are empty and joyless for him."

A well-stated, concise purpose will fill you with new vitality. If you are an older person, it will make you feel though you are youthful again. Your mind and your interests will remain fresh all of your life and, to say the least, you are not likely to enjoy anything more than your work.

You really don't need to become world-renowned or set performance records to be enjoyably and productively engaged in living. You do, however, need a strong commitment to a real reason for being, something toward which you can direct meaningful talent and effort. Such an entity makes the achievement of intermediate goals more attainable and enjoyable. You will even be able to better accept others for what they do.

Let us review the key points of designing a Purpose.

These are the characteristics of a well defined purpose:

1. It challenges you to utilize all of your talents to fulfill that urge within you to do something meaningful for those around you. It will be so meaningful to you that you will be able to imagine it vividly and when clearly stated, it will make you want to work for its actualization.

2. It will cause you to impact the lives of others in meaningful ways. To say the least, it is a valuable service.

3. It is unselfish. Although you will personally derive great benefit from it, it is intended to provide benefits to others.

4. Purpose is intentionally so broad that it will hopefully span your lifetime. You will be engaged in some form of it for as long as you live.

5. You will cherish it because it seems so beneficial. Working toward it will seem so worthwhile.

6. In accomplishing your purpose, life, in some

way, seems to be advanced, at least for some elements of the population.
7. You will seldom tire of performing your purpose. You may possibly join the ranks of those few who say, "It seems too good to be true," or who say "It doesn't seem like work."
8. It is stated simply, usually no more than a few specific sentences.

Not everyone's purpose will extend to universal coverage or even national or regional benefit. Some never extend beyond their local community. Although a neighborhood minister has the capability to reach the heights of a Billy Graham or a Robert Schuler, he may only choose to render his service in his own local community in a local church. The "mom and pop" operators of an enterprise may render a valuable service within their neighborhood, with a view that they are beneficial as they are. The mayor of the local town may never want to be governor.

The McDonald brothers, originators of the McDonald's global fast food concept which has become an institution, chose not to leave the shadows of their homes in California. They gave permission to the late Ray Kroc, a former salesman, to spearhead the expansion of their concept to the rest of the world. The idea may not take the individual outside his hometown, but it can be worthwhile and most beneficial.

Often an idea may blossom beyond expectations. Few ever start out thinking their humble concept can reach the world, but if it does they, like the McDonald brothers, may be forced to decide whether they want to follow it.

Well, you've seen the great value in a well thought-out purpose. I believe it will encompass identifiable talents, causing you to sharpen them and use them effectively.

Overcoming the Overwhelming

God has given them to us for just this expression. Nothing can be more enjoyable and fulfilling than to discover, cultivate and live Purpose. I hope you will use this book to discover yours and develop it.

A purpose statement is your commitment to yourself and to those around you as to why you are here and the service you will render.. It may be as simple a statement as this:

> "My purpose in life is to enhance the lives of others by providing effective leadership in my employment and my family. Upon retirement, I will dedicate the balance of my life to writing and speaking about the principles of life that I learned".

Let me reiterate, your purpose is your statement to the world about what you will do. Don't think so lowly of yourself ever again as to conclude that God placed you here merely to struggle to survive. Imagine the effectiveness, value, and importance of your purpose. Commit to it and flourish.

With respect to the organizational setting, few informed consultants, management scholars, or practitioners would dare think of trying to advise or manage an enterprise without defining and communicating, to as broad a group of concerned persons as possible, the organization's purpose.

Chapter 3

The Self-Image of an Overcomer

A very significant aspect of developing the overcomer's attitude is self, the awareness and development of which we are calling Self-Imaging. Before embarking on this meaningful and exciting journey into mastery over circumstances in your world, it is necessary to spend time exploring yourself or your group. Get to know where you need strengthening and development; come to know a little more about the person you desire to become, indeed, deserve to become.

Many people believe that what they are now is all there is, and they're stuck with it. "I'm going to be realistic"; "I can do no more nor be any more than I already am", they say. The phrase "What you see is what you get", is the by-word of an amazing number of people. So many see themselves as mired and burdened with the self they currently are, erroneously thinking God made them that way. You'd be surprised at the number of people who are angry at God for "making" them the way they are, while all the while they can literally become formidable.

Let's abandon such ideas as ridiculous and vow to

Overcoming the Overwhelming

proceed joyfully to explore the rich and flexible wealth of capability inherent in each human being. Let us come to realize that, to a large measure, we are a great package of raw materials with the right and the commission to develop ourselves into useful entities. Behind all we see, suppose, and become is a God that loves us and is willing to provide His power to just about any claim we make about ourselves. The real criteria for this development is that it is sensible and reasonable to us.

Interestingly, for those who choose to think of themselves as minimal and with little energy to rise above current circumstances, there is power needed and available, to make that choice a reality. Although we won't spend the time in this book to discuss means of actualizing personal weaknesses, it is important to emphasize that it is a personal choice for each of us.

In sharing this concept with you, it is my intent to direct your attention to the marvelous resource inherent in us. I'll provide directions about how to tap those resources, to master circumstances, and move perpetually to higher realities...overcoming whatever confronts us.

Dreaming and imagining is exciting for adults. It's not "just for kids." We don't need to ask permission or feel embarrassed because we dream, imagine, and visualize. In the way we're using this power, it's a lot more than "kid stuff!"

As we pursue this exciting concept, we're not going to be overly concerned about the debilitating factor that we refer to as modesty. Neither will we be overly concerned about appearing immodest. God gave it; it's all right to acknowledge that we have great power and ability.

Strive boldly and confidently to claim the powers that lie dormant within you. Let us focus all our energies on finding workable methods for releasing those powers which give us the authority to become much stronger, confident and talented people. Let's find ways to fulfill the worthy desires nestled deeply in our souls.

Each person is on some plane of life, moving in one direction or another, depending on the set of his mind, the measure of confidence, the strength of his imagination and the soundness of his plans. We are either growing or shrinking, becoming or disintegrating. Always, there is movement. Status quo is purely myth.

Since there will inevitably be movement, you can decide the direction of that movement. How? Consider a poignant statement made by the noted psychiatrist and pioneer in psychotherapy, Dr. William James: "The greatest discovery of all times is that man can alter his life by altering his attitude of mind."

I recall a lesson I learned as a military officer in the field of guided missiles. After the firing of each missile, we would analyze the burst pattern, the burst radius, and other impacts on the target to determine the missile's effectiveness. One point that often arose in this analysis was the "attitude" of the missile in flight. When the burst radius and pattern were within tolerance, we concluded that the missile had the right "attitude." When it was off in its prescribed target parameters, we concluded that it had an improper "attitude", and we proceeded to search for reasons.

One of the frequent assessments of the cause of missile "attitude" was the in-flight direction the missile received from the pre-sets in the computer. Another consideration was how well the missile executed its responses to the commands from the computer.

There are two salient points in this analogy as we relate it to ourselves as human beings:

Overcoming the Overwhelming

1. Do we have the right 'pre-sets' in our minds prior to starting our flight toward our goals?
2. Is there something about ourselves that we should know prior to starting that might hamper our ability to execute en route?

With respect to the first point, is your mind clearly focused and set to the extent that the target (or goal) is reasonably clear and imaginable? Have you taken into account what is required to achieve your goal? Further, will the pre-set information in your mind be sufficient to move you toward that goal? Is the picture of the goal sufficiently clear in your mind that it will move you in the proper direction and sustain you in your movement? Will it keep you motivated?

With respect to the second point, one of the great hindrances to a missile in flight is atmospheric conditions. Often these would be somewhat different from that which was predicted. Sometimes the winds would shift and move at a greater velocity than calculated. Sometimes humidity and air density would be greater than calculated. All of these and other conditions could have an effect on the in-flight attitude of the missile.

We could, however, compensate for most of these automatically. The computer would issue new commands relative to pre-sets, changing the flight and the maneuvers of the missile. But, if the pre-sets were in error, then the new command would be off by a proportionate amount. The missile, due to an improper attitude, would miss its target.

On the other hand, some flaw in its physical makeup, which we usually didn't know about, might cause the missile to execute poorly and thereby miss its target.

In similar manner, poor pre-sets or poor estimations of what it might take to achieve a goal, may cause considerable difficulty once you start out toward a goal. Couple that with obstacles in the environment not anticipated and you have accumulated difficulties that can cause you to miss your goals by a significant margin. This is where the pre-set of an overcomer's attitude can enable you to remain on course.

Starting out with accurate pre-sets or plans, and having a reasonable knowledge of ourselves and abilities are key factors in insuring that we have an attitude which will sustain us in our movement toward our goals, regardless of the obstacles, be they the threat of death or even lesser difficulties.

With this attitude intact, we have a much stronger chance of properly dealing with unexpected adversities and conditions that might occur. All we need to do is call on the creativity in our minds to plot new information so that we can effectively deal with the unexpected and move on. An improper attitude is very likely to falter and cause us to lose orientation or direction, thereby falling short in execution and goal attainment.

It is imperative that we have proper self-knowledge and self-direction coupled with sound plans in order to achieve goals. Before launching, it is important to have them reasonably in place. Therefore, the necessity of developing ourselves into a force of achievement and then setting goals commensurate with the highest realistic estimate of ourselves is of utmost importance.

Let me emphasize that your estimate of yourself must be reasonable. Others may provide valuable impute through criticism, constructive and otherwise, but the final decision about who you are must be yours. To receive this

Overcoming the Overwhelming

vital input from anywhere outside yourself will surely cause you to falter and waver.

Growing up in South Carolina, I lived in a setting that was not conducive to the development of a healthy and positive attitude toward myself. In those formative years, the environment was replete with symbols suggesting that my skin color, which is black, made me somehow inferior. Symbology further suggested that I would probably never equal the achievements of others in the society who were white.

We were required to perform continually those acts which reminded us of our "second class" status—sitting in the back of the bus, steering clear of restaurants, standing back to allow whites to enter doors first, not granted the permission to try on clothing in some stores, attending substandard schools, often being required to say "yasuh" to all white men and "yas'm" to white women, regardless of their ages.

I remember drinking from separate water fountains, adult blacks being chastised and "put in their places" by whites, young and old alike.... On and on I could go, enumerating the symbols which characterized out "second-class" status.

Throughout those developmental years, in spite of the negative conditions, I had a driving urge to be "somebody", as I referred to it. I could not define "somebody", but I burned inside to achieve it. There were days when I, as a young boy, was inspired as I stood at the corner store near my home. I watched what I called white achievers come and go. They seemed so confident and dignified and secure. They seemed to have the "world on a string" as they stopped by to purchase "store bought meat" and sliced bread. It all seemed so wrong for them to have all of the privileges, but I still wanted to be "somebody" similar to what I thought they were.

On other days, I despaired because I knew I wasn't white and I thought I had to be in order to be that "somebody." I didn't realize for many years that the gnawing desire to be "somebody" kept me going and striving. Though generalized, to be somebody was one of my pre-sets.

Besides teachers, preachers, and laborers, there were few role models in my community during those days. My sister was a teacher and my father was a minister, but I found neither profession very interesting. As I went away to college, I had the halfhearted notion of being a teacher.

Once in college, I discovered that it was possible, through ROTC Cadet Training, to become an officer in the United States Army. This intrigued me and for the next four years, I worked very hard to earn a commission as a Second Lieutenant in Army Artillery.

Though proud of my accomplishment on the surface, beneath it all I had a nagging fear that I would "be found out." There was nothing to be found out, but nonetheless I feared the Army would discover I couldn't measure up. In addition, as I entered an integrated U. S. Army, I felt that I wouldn't be able to compete with the white officers academically. I was afraid I would fail and lose my commission as an officer. These fears created a strong sense of insecurity and self-doubt. As a result I moved about nervously and fearfully most of the time.

In spite of this, or because of it, whichever is appropriate, I worked hard and tenaciously. By this means I tended to experience one degree of success after another. My duty assignments during those early years were very likeable and I was given significantly more responsibility than I thought I could handle. But handle it I did. Yet, there

Overcoming the Overwhelming

was always the fear that I wouldn't "measure up" and thereby drown in all that responsibility.

Following a very successful tour of duty in Korea, I thought I had met my "Waterloo". I was being reassigned to a school at Fort Bliss, Texas, to study guided missiles. Having no previous background for this field of study, I simply felt I had come to the end of the line and there simply was no chance for me.

A sociology and economics major such as myself had no business getting involved with missile dynamics, electronics, engineering and operating methods. But, once again I reached within my self, tapped my great resource, and emerged successfully.

Upon graduating from this exciting and enlightening school, my next assignment was to remain at the Guided Missile Center. For two years, I taught guided missiles to senior officers as they studied various strategic and tactical courses relating to guided missile warfare.

This experience was very successful for me. I enjoyed my duties and received numerous commendations for excellent performance. Something still wasn't right. The inconsistency was like a headache that wouldn't go away.

I needed a better understanding of myself. Why did I continue to achieve so well when it was so inconsistent with the negative mind-set I held? I had learned that I could not be successful because of the color of my skin yet here I was achieving. I needed to understand why life was unfolding so well for someone who was so fearful, so insecure, and so void of peace. It just didn't make sense. This needed some re-thinking.

For the first time in my life, I arrested my fears and I discontinued dwelling on my skin color. As I looked at myself as a real person without stigmas or labels, I truly liked what I saw and, amazingly, I found that the one thing that kept me striving and achieving was the gnawing desire to be "somebody."

I was driven to achieve by that desire even though it was not clearly defined. There was that force inside of me that backed me up in whatever I pursued. But whenever I looked into a mirror or acknowledged my skin color, I became fearful that what I saw and perceived about myself would eventually spell my doom. In light of all this, I considered my achievements mere luck or flukes and sooner or later it would all come tumbling down.

At this momentous time of introspection, I finally understood what was happening. I saw that I had everything I needed, in spite of the color of my skin, to be a high achiever. Skin color, I noted, was very superficial. I decided that I could function the same as anyone else.

I further discovered that God had blessed me with every possible personal resource to be an achiever, whether it be low achiever, high achiever or medium achiever. I found it to really be a matter of individual choice. As a result of this discovery, I changed my mind about who I was and my entire life changed. Although I had to fight off the old thoughts and habits relating to my old self-concept, I was able to change my life by changing my mind.

That's worth repeating: *I changed my mind and consequently changed my life.*

I began expecting to achieve. I started demanding it of myself as a matter of course. Above all, I started planning my achievements and imagining them. They happened! The related peace of mind and restfulness was difficult to comprehend.

Maybe you need to change your mind and your visualization of yourself. Perhaps you are missing out on rich treasures because you're hindered by negative thoughts

Overcoming the Overwhelming 51

tucked away somewhere in your mind. Change your thinking and live far beyond what you ever expected. Be an overcomer.

Perhaps you're saying, "But I'm not black so that can't be my problem." Let me point out that being black is only one of countless conditions people focus on to shunt and hamper their growth and negate or limit their prosperity.

There are plenty of crippling stigmas to go around; if one doesn't fit you, another one will. Maybe you're short or very tall. Maybe you're female. Maybe you're simply not very handsome or attractive. Maybe there is some physical feature or limitation that is not acceptable to you. Maybe you're in some way physically impaired.

Any of these, and an endless number of other stigmas, could be hampering you the same as my skin color hampered me. Yes, being black is only one of many conditions people may use to negate their potential. Even some whites use their skin color as a symbol of limitations.

I invite you to join me in this meaningful adventure to determine where you stand and determine what you need to do to unleash your power. I urge you to change your mind to the positive. As soon as circumstances shift, you will experience new life and personal freedom will be on its way to you.

We start this chapter by discussing the procedures for developing a healthy self-image. I'll lead you through the process of constructing a foundation to undergird it. Etch firmly in your mind who you are and what your capabilities are. Don't be one of the many who say, "I must be realistic: I can't do much." That is simply not true. I state firmly: if you follow the guidance given in this book, you will find it so.

As we proceed then, let us define self-image as the way you visualize or regard yourself in your mind. In addition, self-image serves as a blueprint for personal actions. We all have a self-image and most of the time we conduct or manage our lives in accordance with the genuine view or image we have of ourselves. The true self-image is acted out daily, eventually automatically, and, with practice, it expands.

If you are going to manage your life by the principles in this book, you must develop a self-image which assures you that you are capable of doing what you seek to do. You must affirm that you already have the attributes or characteristics needed to bring about what you seek.

Jack Nicklaus, the holder of more golf victories than anyone in history, said he saw the ball going into the hole before he putted, but he practiced thousands of putts per week. In, short, he perceived himself capable of doing what he imagined; by executing it, he developed one of the best styles of play ever performed in the game of golf.

Let us now proceed to describe the steps necessary to build and maintain a healthy self-image.

Step one in the process involves a series of penetrating questions that will serve to open you up. This process will be quite revealing, if you use it properly in being introspective. We are here providing you with some sample questions which may open the process for you. These sample questions are not the only ones you might ask, but they can be very stimulating. They can open you up for even more penetrating exploration. Pore over these questions, and I assure you they'll be very revealing.

Please take a separate sheet of paper and provide answers to these questions on a scale of zero to four with zero meaning that this point is not very often true in your case. A score of 1 implies that only on rare occasions does this point apply to you. The number 2 implies that with some effort this point is true for you. It is true about as

Overcoming the Overwhelming

often as not. A score of 3 indicates that with the exception of some unusual cases, this point is true as you project yourself. Finally, a score of 4 indicates this is definitely a factor in your life.

Read the questions carefully and answer them quickly. Usually your first inclination is the most accurate.

1. I feel I am a person capable of developing a successful and productive life for myself. I can accept others for what they choose to be without any adverse effects on my feelings of self-worth.
2. I accept and welcome appreciation, however, I don't seek it or demand it.
3. I feel worthy and guiltless and relatively free of shame.
4. Generally speaking, I feel good about myself whether I have just completed a task successfully or whether I fell short of excellent results.
5. I am confident I can achieve the goals I have set for myself.
6. I feel I can achieve excellence, admiration and recognition in my chosen field as well as any other person.
7. I look forward to achieving because I have planned it, and I recognize my capability for achieving whatever I seek.
8. I am free to do as I choose; I have that authority. I am controlled only by my sense of right and wrong.
9. I don't hesitate when making decisions. Once I have satisfactory data, I act without fear or worry about what others might think, do, or say, and I am willing to accept responsibility for those decisions.

10. An admission of a mistake or an error does not adversely affect my self-image.

11. I recognize that, like mine, the opinions of others are formulated on the basis of their experiences and therefore do not influence me to any significant degree.

12. Through my expressions I am able to influence the actions of others including those in positions of higher authority than mine.

13. One of my sincerest joys is to see others achieving and experiencing good fortune.

14. I am able to accept people as they are. With some I become friends easily; although I may not become closely attached to certain others, I do not condemn or reject them.

15. I am a listener.

16. I have the courage to live up to my standards and wishes, and I feel no real need or obligation to live up to the standards of others.

17. I think it is necessary to be honest and open even though I recognize occasions when I should consider the feelings of others.

18. I like to give to others because I have a genuine desire to contribute to their well-being.

19. I have a quiet confidence that does not require boasting or frequent display of my material possessions.

20. I have the courage of my convictions, and I can express them without feeling defensive.

Overcoming the Overwhelming

21. My self-image is a product of my choices and achievements. I can change it by taking inventory and redirecting it.

22. I spend time alone simply because I enjoy it and find it necessary. I am also comfortable with others.

23. My sense of security is derived from the way I feel about myself and my abilities, possessions or position have little bearing.

24. I often try to see how things seem to others, regardless of who they are.

25. I trust others until they give me a reason not to.

Total your score and rank them as follows:

86–100   Balanced, wholesome outlook. Mentally healthy and of good spirit. Should be achieving very well. The person sees things positively and usually approaches them with confidence and optimism.

70–85   Good outlook generally. Performance sometimes affected by moods. Performs well much of the time. Self-improvement would not be very difficult.

50–69   Considerably limiting. This person tends to look at things negatively as a matter of practice. Achievements are considerably below potential. May tend to be overly subjective.

50–Below   Seriously limited. Achieves very little. Serious self-doubt. Suspicious of others. Particularly suspicious of those who are different from themselves.

This inventory is a tool of self-examination and nothing more; and I, therefore, urge you to use it as such and not as a clinical device. This questionnaire is to be used to help you get started in the self-examination process.

Whatever the final conclusions, please remember your image can be raised as you begin to work to make changes.

The above narratives will describe where you are currently functioning. In order to recheck yourself at a later time, I suggest you make copies of the questionnaire in the book. This way, you'll have one to use later.

Remember, you're OK no matter what the score indicates. The inventory's only value is to provide some idea as to where you are presently functioning. Before you can begin a journey, you need to know your starting point.

Following the assessment, continue your self-examination by considering the following questions.

a. Are your major concerns your career and your professional health? Where do these rate in your overall life plans?

To check these questions, consider the following factors:

1) Have you developed a personal or group purpose?

2) Identify your significant attributes.

3) What attributes do you think you need in order to succeed?

4) What career plans will enable you to best fulfill your personal purpose, provided you've identified it?

5) As you understand them describe your fears. apprehensions, prejudices toward people different from yourself as well as those in authority.

6) Define personal security, economic and otherwise, as it applies to you. Determine the extent to which you are willing to take risks against it to accomplish what you want.

Overcoming the Overwhelming

7) What is your commitment to family, community, the corporation or organization, church or other elements affecting your life. Have you considered them in any plans you may have?

Please consider these significant questions carefully and thoughtfully assess your answers. Return to them often and rethink them.

As we enter the final exercise regarding personal characteristics, I recommend you consider the following general ones as needed to varying degrees in the lives of all achievers. Measure yourself against these and evaluate them personally, making your decision as to the desired strength of each in your personality. Any one of them can be overemphasized, so please use caution.

1. Ego-drive. The desire to win, persuade, and control others for personal reasons.

2. Empathy. The ability to sense the feelings of others and respond appropriately.

3. Creative Ability. The ability to think of new and different ways of approaching circumstances and solving problems.

4. Boldness. Taking the necessary creative urges that may not fit the norm, aggressively activating them, and seeing them through to fruition.

5. Knowledge. An awareness and understanding of the technology and the processes relating to your life and to what you are doing occupationally.

6. Resiliency. The ability to rebound from setbacks, obstacles and "unfair" results.

7. Flexibility. The ability to stretch and bend a little; to develop compromises and to function appropriately, even if you get a little "mud" on you. The ability to sidestep some issues in order to meet objectives.

It is very important to stress the necessity for developing an appropriate balance between ego-drive and empathy. One without a good measure of the other can be extremely harmful in relationships. Without empathy, a strong measure of ego-drive would likely cause you to overwhelm others in search of victory or in pursuit of your personal desires. In such a state, you would have an obvious disregard for the feelings and concerns of others.

Conversely, a combination of strong empathy and subdued ego-drive would likely cause one to be influenced by the feelings and wishes of others to the extent that your own personal concerns and plans would be disregarded or seriously neglected. Caution must be exercised to insure a healthy balance between those two necessary attributes.

Having considered the foregoing general characteristics that everyone should consider, let us proceed to examine specific characteristics you think you need, personally, to achieve the desired goals you have for yourself.

We all seek to live in some organized fashion. We tend to compartmentalize various aspects of our lives into manageable segments called roles. To know a measure of success in these life segments or roles, we must determine those personal characteristics or traits that will enable us to act in ways which will enhance our chances for success. In other words, if you desire to be effective in a given role, you must take the time to determine the attributes or characteristics necessary for such achievement.

Take a sheet of paper and make several columns

Overcoming the Overwhelming

labeling each role. List each of the roles of your life, i.e., parent, employee (manager, supervisor, etc.), mate (husband, wife, other), friend, neighbor, sibling, professional, son, daughter, and any others that constitute the whole of your life.

Once you have identified all of your roles or as many as you can think of which seem to make your life complete, ask yourself, "What characteristics, in my view, are needed for me to practice these roles effectively"?

List only those characteristics which you, yourself, think are important. Don't permit yourself to be influenced by what others think you should or shouldn't be doing. You must take ownership of each characteristic because it is unlikely you will commit to and practice it with conviction until you do.

I stress this point because it is extremely important. Few of us ever do what others say we "should" or "shouldn't" do effectively until we can bring ourselves into agreement...even if the others are correct. This is very important to a wholesome and comfortable life. It is difficult, if not impossible, to be successfully what others say you should be.

The healthiest people will no doubt be found among those who have come to live their lives in accordance with their own values. If there are certain attributes being foisted upon you by others with which you disagree, you should express your feelings, negotiate with that person and find a healthy middle ground where you both can be comfortable.

If you are not willing to develop all the characteristics you identify as needed to fulfill a particular role, recognize that you won't be very effective in that role, according to your own standards. If you find this to be true, it may be necessary to consider getting out of that role, at least for now.

Let's consider an example before you begin to define your roles.

Role: Parent
Characteristics: (examples of possible choices)
- Authoritative
- Loving
- Leader
- Friend
- Listener
- Considerate
- Open-minded
- Teacher
- Coach
- Understanding
- Decisive
- Disciplined
- Disciplinarian
- Provider

Proceed now to each of the roles you've identified and develop a similar list for each. List as many character traits as you can think of which would describe you in a particular role.

In order to be thorough, this will take considerable thought and time, but it is very important to your success and peace of mind. Take as much time as you need, bearing in mind that you are starting to develop the image of a resourceful, successful and happy person.

After having defined each of your roles, you will probably observe the following:

1. Many of the characteristics will recur in several

Overcoming the Overwhelming 61

roles. Example: The characteristic of listener might be common to every one of your roles. Once you are a listener, it will be the same for every role. Good listening skills are valuable in practically everything we do.

Another example might be loving. This is one that will be common to several roles but it might be acted out differently, depending on the role. To be a loving manager might elicit respect for the employee causing you to encourage the employee, to be considerate of his feelings, and to give him an occasional pat on the back. Being a loving mate might cause you to express intimacies you wouldn't express to the employee. No matter what the acceptable expression, the characteristic behind it is love.

2. Check the characteristics in each of your roles against the following checklist. If any characteristic in any role doesn't fit this checklist, it's probably not legitimate.

    a. Is each characteristic possible for me?
    b. Is it realistic for me?
    c. Is it really necessary?
    d. Do I really desire to express it?
    e. Am I willing to commit to it?

After you have taken the time to answer these questions to your satisfaction, review the characteristics thoroughly. If, based on your judgment, you feel you are reasonably effective already in acting out a certain characteristic place an "X" beside it. Do this for every characteristic in each role.

Now that you have worked on this process independently, and even though you might have consulted with others about certain characteristics, if you find them acceptable you are now ready to confront yourself.

On the basis of the process you just completed, you should be able to say, unequivocally, the following:

> "Each characteristic that defines my roles is *Possible* for me and it is *Realistic*. After careful study of what it takes to be effective in my roles, I truly *Desire* to develop them because they are *Necessary* for me in becoming a successful and achieving person. In those where there is no "*X*", I need practice and I am willing to *Commit* to each".

This is your statement, made by you of your own volition because of the process you just completed. To the extent that you are honest and reliable to yourself, this statement will be also.

Now the important question is, "Are you ready to face it"? If not, that will also tell you a lot about yourself and the extent to which you are likely to actualize your dreams.

The final aspect of this important procedure is very practical. You have now developed a reasonable estimation of yourself and where you are currently operating in your life. Let's proceed to determine what it takes to move from *Now* to *Desired* or, stated another way, from where you are now to where you intend to be at some future time. How does the move take place? The answer is *Practice*, or acting the part.

Before you sleep tonight, or at least during the next 24 hours, you will have the opportunity to practice each of these characteristics.

If you chose listening as a characteristic, you will have a chance to listen to someone. You will have a chance today to show love, discipline, or planning, and so forth. That's the way you have developed your current habits.

Overcoming the Overwhelming

Seize every opportunity, be in constant thought about the groundwork you have laid and practice, practice, practice.

If you should fall short, don't waste time condemning yourself or despairing. Brush it off quickly and start again. Remember, you have decided that these characteristics will signal to the world who you are. Monitor often for feedback, evaluating it and using it to help you become even more effective. You must believe that these attributes will deliver you to the destination you hold in your imagination.

We have gone into great detail in our discussion of self-image development. You will find that it's worth it as you begin to move confidently in the direction of that which you imagine. Never forget that you, and only you, are the instrument of your personal success. You must have an image of yourself that validates the fact that you can and will achieve what you seek. Put another way, you are the deliverer of your imaginings.

We have shared a process which can enable you to change your mind, positively, about yourself...and therefore change your life. The process is perpetual and there is never an end for the aspiring person.

Each of us is who we are because we've made a habit of being that way. If we are to become a different person with even greater and refined capabilities, able to deliver the realities in our imaginations, we must form the habit of being the way we want to become.

The concept is quite simple. It's the associated work that complicates it. I'm sure with the proper blueprint, you'll do it. Work at it consistently and you'll do it.

I close this chapter by reminding you there is no challenge too great, nor any reward out of reach, for anyone who will take the time to understand himself and prepare for the high calling set before him. In the words of Dr. Maxwell Maltz, the noted plastic surgeon and author of several books including *Psychocybernetics,* "Most of us are better, wiser, stronger, more competent now than we realize. Creating a better self-image does not create new abilities, talents, powers; it releases and utilizes what we already have".

To move from *Now* to the *Desired — Practice Practice Practice*

Work at this process daily and you will consistently overcome the overwhelming.

Chapter 4

The Plan —
Something to Imagine

It has been stated in the Bible, "Where there is no vision, the people perish". Similarly, where there is no plan, the people wander aimlessly and will likely be needlessly overwhelmed by many of the circumstances of life.

It is vital that we focus clearly and frequently visualize, in specific terms, that which we wish to be or accomplish. Being able to see it clearly is vital to the overall development of the overcomer's attitude. It sets up an assurance about the future and generates the all important air of expectancy.

I find no better means of focusing than the tried and true method of planning. Planning has long been with us, but used extensively by very few. I commend it to you most highly. For this reason we are incorporating it as the third vital step in being an overcomer.

The primary assumption regarding planning is that somewhere, in some form, all the resources and circumstances you seek are available, and at some reasonable, specified time they will come together into a whole for the imaginative, diligent planner. You must believe this in order to be an effective planner.

In a broad sense, planning is the process of thinking before doing. Essentially, it is making a decision in the present about some future time when certain things will be established in a manner that fits some desirable specification which you consider practical. Further, planning involves taking concepts, needs and aspirations and organizing them into manageable sets of progression. Through planning we exercise our right to dictate our future in precise ways.

As we reflect on planning, we are exercising our God-given right to make our future in some way better — or at least different — from the present.

Many think that planning freezes the future by causing us to be so focused that we miss new opportunities along the way. Although a well conceived plan will be the result of considering all of the facts and logical assumptions about the future, new circumstances and some previously unknown conditions will occur. When they do, the astute planner will adjust appropriately. This is in keeping with one of the characteristics of the plan, that of being flexible.

Although you should hold to the basic foundation and tenets of your plan, you can make adjustments. These changes will be responsive to circumstances that develop and will move you closer to your desired achievements.

If, after starting out with a plan, you scrap the whole thing, my first guess would be that you didn't give sufficient consideration to it before embarking. It is doubtful that a well considered plan will be scrapped completely. Making adjustments, however, is important to keeping the plan realistic.

The basic elements of the plan are goals and action

Overcoming the Overwhelming

steps. The goals might be considered milestones or checkpoints along the way, a series of which make a full plan. Action steps are measures or methods that must be executed in order to achieve the goal. The combination of these, either one set or several, make a complete plan.

The goal is defined as a simplified clear statement of a desired result. The clearer the statement, the easier it is to focus on the object of that statement...and the more easily it can be made the object of desire. The more intense the desire, the better, as you will see later in our discussion on desiring. The clarity, simplicity and realism associated with the goal is important to your ability to focus on it in your imagination and hold it there.

Consider the goal also as the measurable milestone and the action steps as a series of necessary acts to be performed to achieve each milestone. Goals should build toward an ultimate objective, providing the assurance that as you achieve each milestone, you are measurably closer to the objective. Continuing in this way, you can go as far or as high as you want...as long as you execute the action steps.

Because of the individuality of planning, you can decide your own pace and avoid the possible intimidation of someone who might want to move more rapidly. In order for the plan to be realistic for you, you must move in accordance with your abilities and lifestyle.

The same considerations must be made in organization planning. You must consider abilities, knowledge, and available resources when setting your pace. In order for the plan to be effective and believable it must be in keeping with legitimate capabilities and resources.

A well stated goal should specify *What* one wants to achieve. The action steps, when properly spelled out, will specify *How* the goal will be achieved. Here is where considerable thinking, assessment of obstacles, and forecasting enters into the planning process. Of all the possibilities available, what is the best means of achieving it from your perspective?

The question of *When* must also be answered. To respond to it, we must think through and arrive at a specific time frame for achieving the goal. That timing must be realistic to the individual or group doing the planning. Even though you may have to adjust the time as you encounter new circumstances, always assign a time frame to the goal.

When more than one person is involved in the attainment of the goal, the element *Who* must be considered. Wherever possible, identify all of the people who will have a part in the process. Identify all those who will, in some way, be affected by it. Assign specific tasks (action steps) to those who will be a part of the execution and alert those who will be impacted or affected by it.

The answer to *Why* is extremely beneficial to the process of motivation. In the words of Frederick Nietzsche, "He who has a WHY to live can bear with almost any *How*." When given a plausible and exciting reason to accomplish something, most of us will endure far more than ever imagined.

A motivating reason to do something gets the adrenaline flowing, and as most athletes will attest, it causes you to reach far beyond your known capabilities to get it done. Be sure to answer the *Why* question for yourself and for others who will be involved or affected. The reasons for doing something must stimulate all key people who will be involved.

Plans are excellent means of organizing yourself and/or your organization and providing focused direction. If you establish plans objectively, you will be in a position to achieve far more than might be considered possible to one who lacks organization and focus.

Planning also creates an awareness of the vast numbers of possibilities available and, where there is group activity involved—be it family or business—it can be the focal point for group effort and unity.

Planning further demands that you carefully analyze the future, thereby creating a greater awareness of its potentials for you. Planning also provides a springboard to leap from your present condition to the future perspective. It enables you to maximize your possibilities.

Because of the number of possibilities in our complex and multifaceted society, planning is becoming increasingly important to achievers. It is becoming more and more necessary to weave your way through the vast number of possibilities in search of that which is most important to you and your organization.

If, by now, you get the impression I'm trying to convince you that planning is important and vital to the overcomer, you are exactly correct. I have seen and experienced what it can do spiritually, mentally, physically, and materially. During my years as a trainer, I have encountered many people who called the very possible, impossible, because they had not taken the time to ferret out the facts relative to their aspiration.

I have seen people blindly wishing for something that was clearly within their realm of possibility. Because of this they were not able to achieve their objectives, to realize their dreams. Since they hadn't planned, they couldn't see the steps they needed to take. Oblivious to the path, they didn't move along it.

You and I have seen people who could have considerably strengthened their confidence by focusing on a past accomplishment. Instead of calling the accomplishment sheer luck, they could have realized their personal power by saying, "I planned it, set out to do it, and I did it." They were calling their achievement luck because it happened by no specific design.

The saddest commentary of all, however, is the person who has shuffled through life achieving minimally — only to discover when he thinks "it's too late," that he could have fulfilled his dreams, if only he had planned.

There are those who will read this book while resting in a well-defined and comfortable rut. They will declare it so much foolishness or a pipe dream, because such declaration will make them more comfortable in their rut. Many would like to believe they can develop desires and dreams, plan them, and proceed to achieve them. Tragically, their rut has become so comfortable, they can't escape to make changes in their lives.

Yet, on the other hand, there are those who will accept the challenge of the process outlined here, pull it all together, design, and actualize a victorious life for themselves, their families and their organizations. We salute them in advance! They will make the discovery of a lifetime: things are indeed possible beyond their comprehension, beyond their current sense of reality. The investment is self organization and daring to believe and to desire.

To assist you in gearing up to plan something new, or to refine a process you already have, I will outline some characteristics of plans and introduce some other key points. First, the characteristics:

1. Plans should be realistic and attainable.

Work with the elements of your plan until they are

Overcoming the Overwhelming

sensible and practical. Others may doubt your ability to achieve them. However, don't concern yourself with those thoughts. Your plans must make sense to you and those who will be participating with you.

In my seminars I have found people to have the misconception that a plan should be something you never quite reach; that it's always out in the future. This is an error and is possibly confused with *Purpose*, which we said earlier is intentionally unreachable and somewhat idealistic. This description does not apply to planning. The only reason you establish a plan is because you're committed to achieving the various goals associated with it.

2. Plans are concrete and measurable.

Vague plans do not make good vehicles of success. Vagueness has no place in planning. The more solid and sure the actions and definable the goals, the better and more reliable the plan. Thoughts such as "I want a lot of something," "All I can get," or "I want to be great some day," have no place in the planning process. Such non-specific expressions doom a plan to failure. In every possible situation, define your plan clearly and concretely.

The goals you seek, along with the intermediate actions associated with them, should be very evident and definable. The more solid or concrete the better. As you proceed, you should have defined your actions and goals to the extent that you can measure your progress at points along the route. You should be able to assess where you are presently (*Now*) with respect to where you want to be (*Desired*).

When you have achieved a goal, it should be clear beyond any doubt that you've attained it. Because of this concreteness and measurability, you should be able to demonstrate more precision in your future planning.

3. Plans should be expressed in definite time segments.

This is perhaps the most challenging aspect of planning. setting specific and realistic time frames for your achievements should keep you moving briskly. Previously I stressed the importance of stating when a goal should be achieved. Although new information and new challenges may enter into your process, set a time and use all of your discipline and determination to complete it.

When, in all honesty, it doesn't seem realistic or when there are legitimate obstacles that you didn't foresee, adjust it appropriately, always keeping in mind that it is good to move at a brisk pace. This is the best means I know to strengthen discipline and determination.

Enthusiasm is another element that is affected by moving in accordance with your plans. It is a strong force that also affects the flow of adrenaline.

4. Plans should be flexible.

Allow for changes. Leave enough "slack" in your plans to accommodate errors in judgment, the unexpected, and influences that might dictate the need for adjustments or a possible change of course. Don't plan so tightly that, if you encounter an obstacle, the entire plan is in serious jeopardy. Leave room for adjustments.

Allow for possible disappointments. If your plan happens to fail, it's not simply because there are setbacks. They are to be expected and courageously addressed. Build enough flexibility into your plans to allow for mistakes, the unexpected, and even the pleasures you might have. When an obstacle comes along that disrupts your plan, don't allow the frustration to hamper your getting back on course.

Be flexible to the extent that you reserve the prerogative to change your mind about some aspects of your goals or action steps. I am not suggesting that you become whimsical in your planning; that would be counterproductive. However, if you have strong reasons that are supported by sound evidence, then by all means make the change.

5. Plans should be expressed in quantitative terms.

Whenever possible, place a firm, measurable number on your goals. Specify to your satisfaction, and that of the group, *How Much*. How much do you want? How long will it take and *How Many* elements will be enough? Although you might not always assign a number to a goal, especially intangible ones such as building confidence and being happier, always challenge yourself to say *"How Much"* or *"How Few"* in every possible instance.

6. Put your plans in writing and commit to them.

The reason for writing the goal is quite simple. You won't forget it and you can read it over and over, daily, capturing the spirit and essence it had when you first thought it. This is extremely important in maintaining that all important element of enthusiasm. Your commitment is your promise to yourself that you will *Do As You Said*.

Commitment is a test of your personal honesty to yourself. The most vital question is, can you hold yourself to your commitments? Remember that a plan is an organized means of self-development and self-actualization. Write it so that you can have documented evidence of each.

Here are some examples of a goal statement that you might find useful. These statements should be shaped by the crucible formed by the six preceding characteristics:

I will become Manager of a production team by September 30 this year.

We will achieve a production rate of 10,000 pieces per hour on lines A and C by January 31.

In order to amass the $20,000 we need for a down payment on our new home, we will, beginning September 1, save $4,000 per year ($167.50 each pay or $335.00 per month). We will, at this rate, be able to make the purchase by Christmas in six years.

We (*XYZ* Company) will achieve a net profit of 5.5% on total sales of 100 million dollars four years from now.

In order to specify the *How* of a plan it is sometimes necessary to resort to the Idea-generation and Prayer and Meditation segments of this process. Using these approaches will empower you to receive certain action steps and creative ideas needed to complete your plan.

There is usually a nuclear set of action steps which are standard or obvious but you may need to Idea-generate and pray and meditate to complete the full range of action needed to achieve your goals. In other instances you may be required to do extensive research to bring your entire plan together. Whatever is needed, be calm, expectant and patient; you will get what you need.

To begin your planning, begin with simple goals and build on these as your confidence about the process strengthens. If you are already a planner, use the steps mentioned previously to build on. It might be worthwhile to begin by establishing about five goals that can be achieved in the short term. Work at them very carefully, observing everything that happens in the process. If you have established a purpose, I recommend you do this within the framework of that purpose.

Next, prioritize your goals by assigning them a sensible order of achievement. If the achievement of one goal facilitates the achievement of another, then by all means you want to achieve the facilitating goal first. That, in simple terms, is what we mean by prioritizing.

Finally analyze your goals by raising the following questions:

1. Is the goal worthwhile and in keeping with my principles and morals?
2. Is the goal consistent with my overall plan and does it fit the purpose I have developed for myself?
3. What price must I pay in terms of:
   a. time
   b. money
   c. effort
   d. family and personal sacrifice?
4. After determining the price in number three, ask yourself: "Am I willing to pay that price?"

With regard to question number four, if you answer in the negative, you should abandon the goal or, at least, go back and adjust it. It is not likely you will achieve it if you're not willing to pay the price you estimate. This is the same as commitment; you must be willing and committed.

Once the plan is reasonably in place and properly analyzed, believe it completely and know that it is possible, sanctioned by God Himself, and therefore very right for you. You insured this as you went through the process of establishing it.

Believe this completely and prepare to proceed with abandon and with the boldness that comes with true commitment and conviction. The true overcomer does not run about as though "walking on eggs." He is sure, confident and his mind is clear of most doubt and apprehension. What he has planned, he is able to visualize clearly, execute vigorously and expect wholeheartedly.

Without question there will be obstacles, miscalculations and errors, and perhaps serious setbacks en route to the achievement of your goals. Through use of the planning process, you are prepared for these and you can overcome them.

By planning, you can bring your hopes and aspirations into focus, generating the strong anticipation that is the forerunner of excitement and great joy. There can seldom be peace of mind or joy while one is in clutter. Planning helps you master the clutter and bring out your possibilities like a magnet separates small iron filings from sand. Plan your life, visualize your plan and know joy and excitement that might have been previously unimaginable.

When you are tossed on the stormy seas of life, pull out your plans and choose the calmest waters and most desirable harbor. There will always be a wind at the back of the planner. You will have "breaks" that move you along and, through planning, those breaks will always have meaning. Remember the words of a great writer who said, "A ship that does not know what harbor it is making for, no wind is the right wind." Such will never be true of the planner.

As you review planning, try to remember always these ten elements of explanation to keep planning in perspective:

Overcoming the Overwhelming

1. Planning gives your inner power a blue print for achievement.

2. It is the best known way of organizing your life.

3. It is an excellent forerunner of time management.

4. Planning makes the "impossible" seem possible.

5. Psychologically, Man is a goal-seeking being. That is the way he's structured. Using his goal-seeking mechanism for things that are desirable stirs in him powers he would not ordinarily know.

6. Planning is a systematic way of manifesting the desires of the heart.

7. Attempting to actualize things that are too large to comprehend causes mental confusion, frustration, and lethargy. Planning helps break large problems or projects into manageable pieces.

8. A workable, realistic plan diminishes stress and tension.

9. Goal-setting enables one to see his potential and abilities more clearly and use them systematically.

10. Planning enables one to feel mastery over self and circumstances.

Chapter 5

Desire —
The Motivator

Desire is an extremely important ingredient to being an overcomer. It is the emotional element that produces adrenaline. Adrenaline is an agent in the body which, when produced, fires the individual with energy and resolve which he would not ordinarily know. Desire seems to be that element which causes individuals to reach beyond their previously supposed limitations and achieve at heights new to them.

A youthful seeker of success and good fortune set out one day in search of a great and well-known sage. This sage was known to be located near the seashore in a far away city. Several days of travel would be required to reach the city. The journey would take the seeker across rough terrain in intense heat. Considering his desire to know the truth of success, the young seeker considered this a small price to pay. It would be worth the benefits he would realize from gaining the valuable knowledge he sought. As he endured the rough terrain and the intense

Overcoming the Overwhelming

heat, the seeker was kept going by the great promise awaiting him.

After days of travel and near exhaustion on several occasions, the young seeker could see the sage's cabin in the distance. As he approached it, he was overwhelmed with joy. He now began to move briskly and excitedly across the remaining desert terrain. Upon arrival, the young man had to take his place in line. There were numerous others there seeking the wisdom and advice of this well-known man of wisdom and insight.

The young man waited several hours for his turn. Eventually, the time came for him to have an audience with the sage, who was tall and rugged looking and generally a very imposing figure. The young seeker was awed by this intimidating figure. Nervously, he posed his question, "How do I go about achieving great success in my life?" To which the sage responded abruptly, "follow me." With great expectancy the young man followed as he was led down toward the sea.

They crossed the hot, sandy beach and continued walking briskly into the water, until the water was nearly to the young man's chin and just under the sage's shoulders. This seemed a strange circumstance to the young seeker, but he stood firmly as he anticipated the next step in the process of finding the truth he sought.

At this point the sage reached out and placed his hand on the head of the young seeker and abruptly forced it under the water and held it firmly there. The young man struggled helplessly under the pressure of the sage's hands. As the sage felt the young man go limp under his hand, he released the pressure and allowed him to raise his head above the water.

Gasping for breath and visibly shaken, nearly to the point of panic, the young seeker went into a tirade saying:

"Old man, are you some kind of a fool? What in the world is wrong with you? You nearly drowned me! I've traveled this long distance seeking your advice and wisdom and you try to kill me!"

When the young man had completed his outburst, he began walking as hurriedly toward the beach as the rough waters would permit. As he neared the shore, the sage called out to him in a loud, strong voice and asked, "Young man, when you were under the water, what was the one thing you desired more than anything else?"

The startled young man replied, "Why I wanted to breathe, you old fool, what do you think I wanted?" The sage responded with a serious scowl on his face, "When you desire success as strongly as you wanted to breathe while under that water, you shall have it. That's the secret of success."

When you have a consuming desire for success, it will be yours. Total focus on a plan with obsessing desire is the next ingredient in our formula for being an overcomer.

Desire is of paramount importance to our success and achievement. Perhaps you've heard it said, "If you want something badly enough, you shall have it." Other statements to this effect are "Once I have set my mind to something, I usually do it." If this be true, why are so many deprived of the things they want?

Most of us, fearing we might be disappointed, weaken our potentially strong desires into mere wishes and passing fantasy with such expressions as, "I'm not going to get myself all worked up, because if it doesn't happen, I'll be disappointed." It is the "working up" with desire that insures we get that which we make specific.

That emotional involvement in our desires plays a tremendously significant part in our achievements. With-

Overcoming the Overwhelming 81

out the emotional thrust, most of our achievable dreams and aspirations become limp, halfhearted wishes.

The type of desire we are discussing must be strong. Thoughts, emotions, and goals become intermingled to the point that they produce great energy within the person. This co-mingling generates fantastic power driving us toward achievement.

Where a clear purpose or clear goals have been formed as we've discussed them in this book, emotion-based energy can be constructively channeled, creating a dynamism that will not be denied as you move toward your purpose or goal.

Whatever you reasonably consider your success to be, you can attain it — provided you're willing to make it the object of burning desire. After developing a practical purpose and making a clear decision to move ahead confidently, you are ready to execute vigorously.

The more you imagine the objective and the more you execute, the stronger your desire becomes...and subsequently your resolve. Desire is the prime mover, or motivator, in everyone. It is the force that has accompanied every worthwhile achievement.

The biblical character, Job, who was beset with so many difficulties and extreme losses in his life, summed it all up by saying "The thing which I have feared is come upon me." Job's fear thoughts were so intense that his creative mechanism brought them into his life. That is the means by which our system operates. It brings into our lives that which we hold in our thoughts with consistency and focus.

In similar manner as Job, those who have strong desires and are willing to vigorously execute the actions dictated by their creative minds will, on some grand and glorious day, be able to say: "The things I greatly desired have come upon me." No matter what their nature, thoughts create after their own kind.

Researchers and writers such as the noted researcher, Dr. J. B. Rhine of Duke University and Claude Bristol, author of *The Magic of Believing*, have given us the benefit of some conclusions drawn from their extensive study. One significant point is that we tend to stimulate internal energy forces according to their "pitch, intensity, depth of feeling, emotional quality and level of vibration."

An analogy is made between the human mind and a radio, whereby the wavelengths and wattage of a radio station are similar to thoughts and mental energy waves in serving as controlling forces in relation to their constancy, intensity and power.

"Creative force comes," says Bristol, "only when there is a completely rounded out set of thought, when there is a fully developed mental picture, or when the imagination can visualize the fulfillment of our ambition and see in our minds a picture of the object we desire — a house, a car, a career or a condition, and so forth — just as if we already possessed them. Thoughts of one nature stop or overwhelm others — and you readily appreciate how the more powerful and concentrated the thought, the quicker its tempo, the greater its vibration, the more it sweeps aside the weaker vibration, the more rapidly it does its creative work."

In this regard the human body does not know the difference between a real or imagined circumstance. Take for an example, the last time you were hungry and your mind hungered for a specific meal. As you began to think intently about this imagined meal, your taste buds enlivened and your body actually secreted juices to aid in digesting this meal even before you got it.

In our affluent society, most of us need only to go out

Overcoming the Overwhelming

and purchase this meal and eat it. But just think, if times were difficult and you were not able to so readily procure the meal, you would now be driven to find it and the odds are that you would. You would become very creative in finding means of getting this dish.

Substitute meals didn't appeal to you the same way. Even though you ate something else, the urge and hunger remain for that which you imagined. We can reach the point of such intensity that we are actually driven. This applies to anything you desire; if you want it strongly enough, you won't be satisfied with second best.

Desire can extend from mere wishing or lusting all the way to unbalanced craving. I refer to the healthy type of desire as that which is a longing, but yet associated with a will. This combination insures that we have an earnest and legitimate desire which stimulates us to act and to make a firm commitment. Without these we are not likely to make very much happen.

Being an emotion, we can best comprehend the work and function of desire by defining emotion and deriving an understanding of how it impacts the organism. Psychologists generally agree that an emotion is disruption or disturbance, during which time the human organism is temporarily 'out of' or away from planned action. Emotion is the product of the way the individual perceives a condition in his environment based on memory and knowledge, and, as distinguished from organic processes such as hunger, headaches, pain or other internal conditions, known as feelings or moods.

In contrast to these, emotions of fear, love, embarrassment and desire, among others, depend on a person's understanding, memory, attitude and motives. A motive is an element through which the individual is stirred to action.

Desire, then, affects many of the vital elements of the creative and productive processes from thought patterns to neural responses and behavior. Specifically it:

1. Focuses on the thought picture which we hold in our minds and it further causes it to be projected onto the point where the conscious mind and the creative mind of God connects within the individual.

2. As the picture of the desired results is held in focus, there is a vivid and indelible etching of it onto the two minds, which are, in turn, set in motion. The conscious mind is affected because it uses the etched picture to fight off all thoughts of lesser or contradictory pitch when they attempt to enter in and break concentration and focus. The creative mind is set in motion to produce creative ideas which, when executed, will lead us step-by-step to the objective.

In order to understand the vividness of the picture which has been etched onto the creative mind by desire, visualize a prism held in the sunlight. The sun's rays are projected through it onto a piece of paper. The intensity of the heat from the sun's rays will eventually cause the paper to burn.

Similarly, an image held firmly in mind and impacted by the emotion of desire causes a "burning" of that image into the creative mind. The creative mind, in turn, is set in motion to do its perfect and infallible work.

Because of my positive experiences with the creative mind, I am willing to speak in its behalf much the same as Emerson spoke: "The judgment of the subconscious (creative) mind which represent instincts and accumulation of experiences, is virtually infallible, and I would always trust

Overcoming the Overwhelming 85

its decisions over any judgment arrived at through a long and reasonable process of conscious thinking."

3. The forces I've mentioned, being intensely at work in the individual, generate a tremendous amount of enthusiasm which sets him in motion and keeps him there. This new energy will render each of us considerably more active and invigorated. As we keep the pictures of our aspirations clear, we will be continually on the leading edge, producing at an ever increasingly high level.

4. The capacity for self-motivation and excitement begins to characterize us; our lives become significantly different. The full range of our possibilities becomes strangely expanded. Our new levels of curiosity and sense of exploration will forever lead us outward and upward and we begin to see ourselves the way God sees us:an instrument of service, productivity and success.

Desire may also be viewed as the catalyst bringing creative forces together, stirring them into dynamic action. As a result, we continually turn newly created images into realities. We do, indeed, have the elements of success inherent in our being. Each of us in our own way and according to our own design, make things happen; little things, large things desirable or not so desirable things, according to our personal mind sets.

Let us now review the process of developing the emotion of desire:

1. I have strongly urged you to make your purpose statement simple and clear. Further, I have suggested that yourself-image be sufficiently strong to force you to stretch a little. I've recommended that

your plans be clear, concise, and detailed. All of this is recommended so that you can meet the first criteria for desire, which is clarity and simplicity. Generalities and long, complex, philosophical statements tend only to confuse. Generalities such as the following are considerably harmful to the creative process:
a. I want a lot of money.
b. We want to earn as much profit as possible.
c. I want to know God better.
d. I want to achieve something great.
e. I want to do my best.
f. I want to go as far as I can.
g. I want to improve my life.

Such statements have little or no effect in giving direction to the elements of imagination. They will be avoided by the enterprising and creative person, because they merely impede progress. It is necessary to be specific. Besides, it's fun specifying your dreams.

2. Secondly, it is necessary to convert from wishing or day dreaming to vividly desiring. During my years of conducting seminars, it has been my experience that when we lead participants through the process of goal-setting, the majority treat their goals list as a wish list. In short, they don't really involve themselves with their goal statements. They hold themselves back. Most are not willing to settle into the aspirations to the extent of being consumed by them to the point of commitment. Nor do they believe they can achieve them strongly enough to abandon reservations.

The major factor contributing to this is lack of belief,

but that's not really a problem because if you keep focusing on what you've decided you want, the disbelief will fade as the focus becomes clearer. Refuse to accept the impossibility suggested by your self-image, that's simply the doubting, former self trying to hang on and offer you the safety and comfort it once offered you.

If your former self wins, you return to where you were and call all of this effort mere folly. Some of the people in your environment will offer what they call sound advice. Resist it, and the temptation it offers will fade. To convert from wishing to desiring, you must completely involve yourself, mentally, with what you've decided you want. It is also very helpful to convince yourself that you deserve what you are pursuing.

    3. Visualize the benefits of your aspirations regularly. If they are unclear or vague, get pictures, taste or smell something similar to what you are seeking. Go out and experience something similar to what you want and dwell on it. Years ago, as I first began to practice these principles, I would go out and drive the car I wanted to own.

After driving it, I could close my eyes and feel the luxurious interior encircling me or I could recall the new car aroma. These all helped me to work diligently and to persevere until the items I was imagining became realities. If you want to earn high profits in a business, take a profit and loss statement which you find impressive and read over it until you can see it clearly in your mind. If it is additional sales you want, get a few of the checks that have come into your accounting department and stare at them until you can see them coming in as a result of increased sales.

Sense the feeling you'll have when all the things you

want to achieve are done or are under way, hold that feeling and the action steps will come to you and subsequently all the power of the universe will begin to function in your behalf to bring you what you desire. Start feeling the elation and the comfort now that will be yours later.

Again I urge you to focus regularly on the benefits to you and to others. Your creative mind is systematically being impressed by your vivid images and messages. This is where you want to get it all because this is where the significant action takes place.

Work diligently on your worthwhile desires, because it is this desire that will cancel out the recognition or acceptance of impossibility. When you refuse to accept impossibility, faith begins to develop and certainly is the foundation for your achievement and ultimate success.

Through faith, with its unusual powers, miracles happen. Things will happen for which there seems to be no explanation. Faith can best be described as a firm and positive conviction that permeates your being, setting all of the laws of attraction in motion and, in turn, enabling the predominant or vividly imagined thoughts to link with their objects.

Napoleon Hill, the author of the classic book on achievement titled *Think and Grow Rich*, summed up the power of desire quite succinctly in these words: "I believe," he says, "in the power of desire backed by faith, because I have seen this power lift men from lowly beginnings to places of power and wealth. I have seen it rob the grave of its victims. I have seen it serve as a medium by which men staged a comeback after having been defeated in a hundred different ways."

Hill goes on to say, "I have seen it provide my own son with a normal, happy, successful life despite nature's having sent him into the world without ears."

Overcoming the Overwhelming

Desire instills great power in us all. For this reason, I urge you to pay any price, or cross any hurdle to attain it, because it is a pearl of extremely high value. I, like Napoleon Hill, have seen it work in many spectacular ways to bring about unfathomable success.

Chapter 6

Idea Generation — An Endless Process

Return with me for a moment to the turn of the twentieth century, the beginning of the industrial onslaught in America. You would in all probability be riding in a horseless carriage, earthbound, with no means of communication across long distances beyond that which your voice could reach. In retrospect, the era would appear to be the era of inconvenience.

There were no compact discs, no VCRs or microwaves. The very thought of a computer would probably have terrified us, causing us to strongly persecute anyone who would dare suggest such a concept. Copying documents or even typewriting them would be far from our minds. There is no blender, no electric light, farm implements are in their crudest state and the railroads are just developing and there are no indoor toilets.

It is frightening to think of such a period and one wonders how the people of that day survived. We become quite glad that we live in this era of convenience and the global fast life.

But did you stop to wonder how man has advanced to the remarkable age in which he lives? It was by idea generation and vigorous execution. We must come to accept the fact that, like God, we are creators and have not yet begun to see what lifestyles are possible as we use our creativity to advance life even further. It will happen you know.

It will not take nearly a century again to advance as far as we have over the last century. Creativity begets creativity and in just a few short years from now we will far exceed the advances made over the last century. This is due, of course, to certain individuals who will align themselves with the free flow of ideas in the universe, tenaciously formulate them into a plan and execute them with fervor. Now that the forces are moving so rapidly, the survival of the individual depends on his ability to create. Being creative or responsive to ideas is fast becoming a necessity rather than a mere choice.

It might be advisable for each of us to ask ourselves, "If all men used their minds as I use mine, would we be living in this era of convenience and inventiveness or would we be hopelessly mined in the dark ages. The answer to this question might be very revealing to you as you assess your overcomer's capabilities.

When we examine what has happened through the creative abilities of such a few inventive persons, we can see that overcoming the overwhelming is a real possibility for all of us. It has been demonstrated clearly that we, by our design and nature, are overcomers. The problem is that so many of us have allowed ourselves to be overwhelmed by that which we are capable of mastering. Thank God a few people in our history have demonstrated the capabilities inherent in us. They come forth through idea generation. Idea generation, once discovered, is one of the most exciting and fun exercises there is. Besides, it has life-changing and enhancing benefits.

Albert Einstein has given as good an explanation of idea generation as any I've heard. He says: "To raise new questions, new problems, to regard old problems from a new angle, requires creative imagination." Most of us have done this, only to abandon it later. Creative people, however, respect their own ideas and they hang on to them, nurturing them to some level of fruition. They permit their minds to move into unchartered territories, seeking to expand what they already know. The tragedy is that the institutions in our culture so rarely promote creative thinking or idea generation that by the time a person is an adult he thinks he has no capacity for such things. To him the "gifted" is regarded as specially endowed. I am writing this book because I know this situation can be reversed.

As we enter this segment of our process it is appropriate to reiterate that every great invention, human creation, musical score, writing, and poetry, among other endeavors, came from the creative mind which God has implanted in each of us. The price we as individuals pay is to prepare ourselves by vigorously executing the steps presented in this book.

It must be done with considerable care as we keep our creative minds stimulated with the emotion of desire. By this means, we will achieve astounding results, perhaps far beyond expectations. When you get your creative system moving in the proper direction, the power of God will be working with you to keep it moving at just the right pace.

When you start working in harmony with your creative mind, things will fall into place unexpectedly. Sometimes it may even feel as if someone — another intelligence you

Overcoming the Overwhelming

cannot see but whose presence you sense, is walking right there with you.

Often, the results you achieve will amaze you and sometimes overwhelm you. Ideas will come from all directions. When you see these signs, you will know that you've paid the price for getting your creative house in order. Now as the wealth of ideas come, you must trust and obey by boldly and courageously executing according to the purpose and plan you are following. Remember, you must execute. That's what insures continuity. The creative mind will not work properly for someone who will not obey and execute.

Idea Generation is a result rather than an effort requiring considerable attention to get going. Our discussion of it will be for the purpose of making you aware of the demands it places on you in order for you to reach your goals. If you have designed a healthy self-image, hammered out a purposeful statement, have plans you've worked on in accordance with our suggestions, you will get a steady flow of ideas.

In my personal experiences, I have come to the conclusion that, from a spiritual and an idea point of view, all is in abundance. Those who choose to attune themselves to and walk closely with God will see that all things are indeed abundantly supplied and that all things are possible.

Your immediate reaction to such a statement might be, "Why don't all people experience this abundance?"

It is my honest belief that most of us are out of tune with what God intended for us when He created us. We have drifted far off course from the station in life where we were intended to operate. I would speculate that fear and desire for security are major factors marring the great possibilities and potentialities in our lives.

This fear is not a design feature, because the Bible tells

us that "God did not give us the Spirit of fear, but of power and of a sound mind." Man has drifted away from his calling to be creative to a point where, on the average, he has become dull and marginally productive. This does not mean, however, that he is not abundantly supplied with ideas which would perfectly solve problems, overcome obstacles and supply all his needs as well as desires.

Ideas for creativity and achievement flow to us constantly. It is only fitting that one of the most creative and inventive people ever to live, Thomas Edison, remarked, "Ideas come from space. This may seem astonishing and impossible to believe, but it is true. Ideas come from out of space." This wasn't a theory with Edison. He proved it as no other person has by doing the impossible over and over in so many ways.

Through *Idea Generation* plans are developed, problems get solved, lives are made whole, and new conveniences are invented. On and on we could go enumerating the effects that we can have on life when we permit the ideas generated in the creative mind to flow into consciousness.

As these ideas flow, they are charged with solutions to problems. One by one they lead us to correct courses of action which, when followed, direct us to results never imagined. Many people, including Carver, Edison, and others would verify this assertion. In following the readings of the creative mind, we should not hesitate or be hampered by reservations. Once we receive the idea and examine it to understand what it means, we should act with confidence and courage.

Each situation or aspiration that arises has several possible approaches. Consciously, we are focused on the norms and restrictions of our culture. Consequently, we are aware of numerous limitations which cause us to be unaware of the many possibilities in the creative mind.

The creative mind does not suffer this delusion of limitation and is therefore free to generate unlimited ideas in response to a need, a desire or the urge to create something new.

Designed into our brain is one of the most efficient and capable computing systems ever developed. Because God is the builder and the sustainer of this system, it can be expected to function perfectly and completely in providing better solutions and urgings than any that could ever be generated in man's consciousness. Some refer to this system as intuition, creativity, or leadings. Whatever the name, it is ours, designed into us to take us wherever we want to go to enjoy the lifestyle that can be ours.

The ideas and urgings that come from this computing system must be inserted into our plans at the appropriate place. Actions associated with them must be executed vigorously. This computing system can be seriously hampered and rendered virtually ineffective by an excessive amount of logic and reason. Logic and reason are not detrimental elements in themselves; but, when they lead you to believe that where you are currently functioning is, by far, the best place to be, you are using them excessively.

The intuitive or creative side of us is not always given to significant logic. Because this creative mind is inductive, an event need never have happened before and yet our creative system can lead us to completely new results that defy logic and reason.

A review of the great works in history and the persons responsible for them will bear this point out. Logic and reason have been defied many times in the past. The results have been astounding for those who defied it and persisted in executing their plans. It has, however, been defied far fewer times than it might have been, because too few of us dared to venture into new areas leading to innovations.

The pressure from those around us who do not understand our ideas can be so great as to cause the vast majority of us to continue to live in old ways, remaining on well trodden paths.

In order for you to be effective in using your rich creative mind, you must believe that the idea which you have received can be executed. You must see that it is possible for you, or your group, to do it.

Believing something can be done generates ideas to get it done. Through belief the creative mind is triggered into action. Once belief is focused on a specific result, all the forces of this universe cannot stop the creative mind from generating a string of ideas that will produce results. Execution of the ideas as they come facilitates the flow of other ideas.

When each one is executed and followed, the plan will eventually be brought to fruition. In short, when we look for ideas we will find them. We must believe that answers exist now and we must set out to find them.

There is a well known means of obtaining ideas. We spell them out for you below. Follow this approach and I'm certain you'll have the ideas you need to carry out your plans.

1. Relax and be calm at least ten minutes early in the day, preferably shortly after awakening in the morning. Clear your mind of all matters not related to your plans and first think of the abundance in the world and reflection the assurance that God wants you to have what you seek. Finally, concentrate on the image of that which you seek.

Overcoming the Overwhelming

2. Believe that there is no reason for anything to be withheld from you and the answers you seek are already in fragments floating in the air around you.

3. Act vigorously on every step relating to your purpose and plans, no matter how simple it may seem. Once you've determined it's right for you and fits your plans, do it; make a real point to act on it.

4. Spend some portion of your day examining the opinions of others and note carefully the effects they are having on your personal motivation. Some opinions may obviously be discounted and rejected, while others many have merit and thereby complement your overall plans. Weigh each point that seems to have merit.

5. Set aside time each day for questioning and analyzing your old system of logic, old habits and your present way of doing things. Ask yourself: "What's the worst thing that could happen to me if I discontinued this or that action completely?" You may be pleasantly surprised to know that in many cases if you changed your habits and customs, things might get better. Even if they got no better, you'd be better off for simply making the change. Each day try to do one thing differently. All of this creates new molds for generating new ideas by which you can systematically move in fresh directions. This is true no matter how good and desirable things may currently be.

    This process keeps you out of a rut. It insures the flow of vitality into your life as it leads into new areas for discovering possibilities in your life. You may begin by doing something as simple as taking a different route to and from your place of work. It may be enlightening to know how dull our lives can become when we do the samething over and over. It destroys the sense of adventure through which innovations are developed.

6. Upon becoming disappointed, discouraged or otherwise stymied, remind yourself as often as you need, that the creative force within cannot fail. If things are not very dynamic at this time, it's only a lull period. If you persist, you will rise again to your peak.

Everyone will have periodic valleys. Be sure yours are temporary by determining that they will go away. The pull of discouragement can sometimes be overwhelmingly strong, but this is your chance to demonstrate that you are greater.

At all times remember that the creative mind did not bring you to this low ebb and you will not be forsaken while you're there. You have arrived at that point that you may learn something. Be quiet, learn it quickly and move on, vowing not to arrive at that same point again. This vow can be kept through right action.

7. As often as you think of it, transfer your focus from yourself and its limitations to the creative mind that is in you and its omniscience and omnipotence. Think of its limitless possibilities. Think of the great amount of power that is yours because this mind is present in your life. Realize that you are becoming more and more attuned to its capabilities.

Overcoming the Overwhelming

8. Stimulate your imagination and recall images of what you sought as often as you can, the more the better. However, you should not permit this action to interfere with your productivity.

9. When faced with problems, be positive about your ability to solve them because you know that somewhere in space there is an answer and if you persist, it will make its way to you.

10. Be prepared and available to execute in accordance with your ideas at all times.

11. Maintain a mind of gratitude and humility, thanking God that you are far more capable than you thought you were. Appreciate how you are getting even better gaining confidence as you act on the ideas that come your way.

The person who endeavors to follow these eleven suggestions will generate ideas beyond what he imagined, marveling at the fact that he is capable of so much more than previously thought. Do this for a lifetime and you'll realize there is no limit.

Working in conjunction with each other, emotions and ideas are formidable, with the emotions being the prime force for the execution of ideas. Dr. Maxwell Maltz, in his book, *Psychocybernetics*, tells us that: "Thoughts and feelings go together. Feelings are the soil that thoughts and ideas grow in. Therefore we advise you," he says, "to imagine how you would feel if you succeeded — then feel that way now." This is the best known means of idea generation.

Chapter 7

Pray Without Ceasing

Prayer & Meditation — A Link with the Divine

We come now to the most intriguing and possibly the most powerful element of being an overcomer. All that we have discussed here is predicated on a firm and effectual foundation of prayer and meditation. Without these elements, all we've said would be superficial and of minimal effect. A consistent and meaningful inclusion of prayer and meditation in a life gives vitality and power to that life and keeps the individual growing and overcoming.

Significant achievers, as well as those whose achievements are moderate, attest to "that something that comes to their rescue in times of need." Some leave the explanation of "it" in the realm of the mysterious, while others have systematized a workable procedure, becoming very specific about who "it" is to whom they are praying. So many of the specific persons refer to this "something" as God.

Overcoming the Overwhelming

In the Bible there is the statement that "The effectual, fervent prayer of a righteous man availeth much." That is to say that the valid or legitimate prayer, prayed with emotion, by a person who is thinking rightly (with faith) produces great results. I can attest to this; it works consistently for me as well as many others whom I've interviewed. Alexis Carrell, a medical doctor and research scientist, in spite of all of his scientific insights, took time to write a book, *Reflections On Life*. In this book, he comments on the mystical subject of prayer. He says:

> "The effect of prayer is usually a positive one. Things happen as if someone, God, heard us, had compassion and answered. Things occur beyond expectation and, while in prayer, an equilibrium is established and that which seemed chaotic is balanced and stormy seas seem calmed. In effectual prayer our apparent lack of strength and potency will disappear and our sense of uselessness of effort seem to be erased. In prayer, the cruelties and coldness of the world can be seen from a new perspective and somehow manageable."

It has been my experience that the weak is strengthened and the hopeless is restored to hope. From our time of prayer and meditation we will emerge with assurance and a power that penetrates the depth of our being.

From the words of Dr. Carrell we might conclude that prayer and meditation is the foundation for the overcomer. In his words, prayer brings all that is needed for living with mastery. It gives hope, power, restoration, even assurance and expectancy. The requirement is that we pray fervently and effectually. Certainly anyone who harbors any thoughts about the correctness of these claims would want to engage in prayer and meditation.

I hasten to point out that we will not concern ourselves with posture, religious affiliation, chants, formats, or other such considerations. In our view these are not important. Although I cannot fully explain or grasp how prayer really works, I can say that man, in addition to being physical and mental, is spiritual. Much of what we have discussed so far has related to the physical, but prayer is a direct link to the spiritual and it creates harmony between man and the divine, however he perceives it.

In all of my research, I have not found anyone who fully understands how prayer works...but many attest to the fact that it works and produces results. Prayer doesn't change God or His spirit, but it does, in fact, change us as well as our circumstances. I have staked my life on it and found it to be sufficient.

I don't know where you are on the issues of the spiritual but, as Dr. Carrell points out, the spiritual is a vital aspect in completing the reality and wonder of life. There is enough evidence to underscore the fact that it is central to invention and intuition.

From our time in prayer and meditation, we should achieve an overall perspective that makes the heretofore unmanageable seem manageable. Weakness is overcome by a sense of strength and, above all, the person who maintains a consistent program of prayer and meditation senses a strong link, indeed, a link to the divine.

Although this oneness is not conscious or intellectual, we can feel it. We nurture it by faith. The result of this linkage is that the power latent within each of us is brought to the surface and we have the authority to focus it on the objects and conditions that are meaningful to our lives.

Throughout this book I have mentioned if often, but it bears repeating: the universe contains an infinite number of possibilities and promises. We marvel at the current achievements in our history, but we have barely penetrated the surface in discovering the range of human possibility. I truly believe that the hopes of mankind rest on his creativity as he relates to the divine. In spite of all our accomplishments, we are living far beneath what is possible — both personally and as a society. What we see is a very small part of the full reality of the divine.

Each of us would do well to have a frequent taste of what the world of artists, musicians, philosophers, scientists, and inventors see as they search for solutions and possibilities. We need to see that by faith we can be inseparably linked with the divine and that we can, through prayer and meditation, ask pertinent questions and derive the full benefit of divine wisdom.

From this linkage with the divine we can develop a relationship that consistently empowers and propels us along a path to our goals and purpose. Additionally, we would see that there need not be any weakness in us and that the vicissitudes of life, whatever they are, are under our power.

It is important to point out that I am not advocating a religious involvement. True, it is good for each of us to have such an involvement as it can serve to guide us and discipline us in our development of the spiritual aspect of our lives. But that's not my purpose. Regardless of fundamental thinking on the subject, prayer and meditation works for all of us. On this basis, I advocate it; it is the spirit of a person that truly sustains him. It keeps him fresh and full of vitality when he regularly attends to it. The full range of the positive results of an effectual prayer life are unlimited.

In our culture, prayer and meditations runs the gamut from loud yelling and exhorting of a seemingly reluctant God to peaceful and restful communion and reflection. Whatever the manner, the ultimate intent should be oneness and ever increasing power. Behind it all is the intent to maintain a strong sense of awareness of our divine power and presence and to live holistically and productively.

It is also important to point out that the prayer that we are discussing might be quite different from ceremonial prayers such as those performed at religious ceremonies and other public meetings. One should express himself in prayer in a much less formal or wordy manner. Interestingly, when his disciples asked him how to pray, Jesus responded with a short, concise, sixty-six word example which we now call the "Lords Prayer." In this sample prayer, Jesus affirmed significant points about the individual's affiliation with the divine as well as what he could expect to receive.

Regardless of your attitude toward religious involvement or affiliation, prayer and meditation is strongly recommended if you are to enjoy the benefits of a healthful and creative life. It seems that the divine intent is for us to live in this imaginative way.

Much has been written by reputable scholars and practitioners on the subject of prayer. I feel that many of their points are significant. However, I choose to make reference to the Bible, because it offers some salient, simple points from the most powerfully spiritual person I know of, Jesus. Because of this, I will draw from its pages concepts that I think beneficial to our development as overcoming individuals.

Prayers, with a negative or positive focus, right or wrong, are answered. The tragedy is that, unknowingly, we often pray for negative results, and the prayers are answered. Because of this, it is important to be aware of what we are calling prayer.

When talking with his disciples one day, Jesus said to them, "That men ought always to pray, and not to faint." At another point in the Bible, the Apostle Paul urges his

Overcoming the Overwhelming

followers to "Pray without ceasing." How, I ask, can we adhere to these instructions and ever expect to get anything done if prayer is a formal act or a matter of posture? I believe it is none of these, but rather one's strongest and predominant thoughts are knowingly or unknowingly his prayers. Yes, what we fervently hold in our thoughts are prayers.

To pray without ceasing implies that we are praying for something all of the time. The consistent and regular thoughts that we harbor come to fruition. This suggests that we must exercise discipline in our thought patterns and develop clear thoughts if we are to achieve the object of our desires. The undisciplined pattern of thinking to which many of us subscribe comes to fruition in our lives. Whether we like the results or not, we are receiving in a manner consistent with our predominant thoughts.

In order to insure that we have the correct thoughts, a plan with clear goals is valuable. If we truly desire our goals, we should think of them constantly, thereby praying without ceasing.

Earlier we said that "the effectual fervent prayer of a righteous man availeth much." The word fervent suggests strong feeling, devotion, or earnestness. It relates to the word desire, which is a strong feeling and a devotion for that which we have included in our plans. If we pray or think with this fervency, much will be availed to us. This book's chapter on desire has this concept in mind. With desire, the elements of your plan can more easily be held in your prayers.

When we are able to develop strong desire and hold tenaciously to the elements of our plan in our minds, we will be amazed at the results. Merely overcoming will be an understatement!

Another relevant quotation from the scriptures which

I find very interesting and inspiring reads: "And this is the confidence we have in Him, that if we ask anything according to his will He hears us, and we know that if He hears us we have the petitions we desired of Him already." This statement is worth rereading.

This statement does not equivocate. It is precise and clear, leaving nothing to be read into the lines. The part that says "according to His will" has so often been taken to mean, if He wants to do it; as though God is a celestial string puller deciding what we should or should not have. I believe this to be in error. I believe it to mean that you must pray in accordance with the laws of the universe. In short, my thought on this is that as an example you should not expect to get positive results if you are praying for gravity to alter its function and simply permit your body to go sailing in the distance.

If by faith, you know your prayers to be heard then you have that for which you prayed. Be sure it is in line with the order of things. This is why I advocate acting "as if." As if you have already received. If you are sure your prayers are heard, then that which you prayed for is in the making.

Another element to be mentioned here is that of faith. We must have it with our prayers. Faith is the element that makes us know that there is someone greater than we who are praying. Faith also suggests that He hears us. It is impossible to comprehend the one to whom we pray so we must believe that he exists. Additionally, we must believe that he is willing to respond without a lot of strings and other entanglements. The exercise of prayer, then, from beginning to end is by faith.

We will define faith as placing trust or confidence in some person, thing or condition, whether there be objective evidence or not. In spite of the initial lack of objective evidence, we believe in a power greater than we are. At the beginning of the prayer process there will be little or no evidence. Pray anyway, and as you begin to see the results, your faith will be strengthened to the point of eventual expectancy and certainty.

An oft quoted scripture that is in line with what we are saying here is, " Now faith is the substance of things hoped for, the evidence of things not seen." Faith is the stand-in for that for which you are praying until it comes into reality. We treat faith as if it is the real object. The true believer who prays is often misunderstood because he holds tenaciously to something that he fully believes exists in his mind. Many such persons have been scorned and considered "crackpots" because they believed so strongly in what they expected. People around them simply could not understand.

Creative people press unswervingly for objects and conditions because in their minds it is real. When everyone else wants to abandon the aspiration or the concept, the person of faith sees it clearly and wants to press on even in the absence of objective evidence. Faith makes the dream or aspiration substantive and ultimately real. Finally we could conclude that faith is the total absence of doubt.

So often we look beyond these assurances and exercise our freedom to develop superficial explanations for why we are not achieving or why we are overwhelmed. Such explanations as lack of education, lack of talent or ability are chosen when all the while we could be delivered to great achievement if we would but develop a plan and pray and exercise faith about that plan. Through prayer and faith thoughts of limitation diminish, thus releasing the individual to find that which he needs to do what is necessary to become or to do what he wants. The truly committed, believing person is frequently doing the seemingly impossible.

With a clearly established self-concept and goals, we can avoid daydreaming and wishful thinking. Such tendencies are then replaced with dynamic and creative action. Having arrived at this state, we don't simply hope or wish, we know. Instead of pleading in our prayers, we proclaim. We genuinely expect that which we declare to come about in our circumstances.

Realizing that our thoughts are prayers, we must become vigilant about the thoughts we entertain. Our predominant thoughts set in motion the spiritual forces that bring change.

Whether we attend churches or synagogues or not, we can lead prayerful lives, and I commend it to you highly. Whether we are "believers" in the traditional, religious sense or "non-believers," our thoughts are prayers and they move or affect the universe bringing results commensurate with those thoughts.

In addition to praying for ourselves we need to pray for others, making sure our prayers are in line with their earnest desires. It is imperative that we know what they want, otherwise we will not pray in harmony with them and therefore little is likely to happen. In the scriptures a blind man came to Jesus asking him to have mercy on him. Jesus did not assume because the man was blind he wanted to see. In order to insure he was working in harmony with the man's wishes, Jesus asked, "What wilt thou have me do unto thee?" Most of us would have thought it obvious what the blind man wanted. Not Jesus, because he knew the mechanics of prayer. Praying for others also strengthens your prayer life.

No matter what others may receive you will not be hindered from getting what you want. An unselfish atti-

Overcoming the Overwhelming

tude is very beneficial. Additionally, praying for others sets up a right relationship and union which leads to a stronger awareness about how we are joined together.

There are numerous ways to enter into a process of peaceful and quieting prayer and meditation. The approaches are too numerous to mention. I considered several to share with you in this book. I find the following ones to be most effective:

1. Follow the steps we have mentioned so far, writing your concerns, aspirations and/or problems as clearly and completely as you understand them. You only need to cover the complete format one time. From then on it is a matter of inserting changes as they occur. Examine what you have written, questioning yourself completely and thoroughly.

2. Being satisfied that you've stated the problem, concern or aspirations clearly, begin visualizing the conditions and solutions most practical and satisfactory to you. Get them firmly fixed in your mind, believing that there are answers far beyond your comprehension.

3. Clear your mind by dismissing the thoughts you just considered. Start the prayer and meditation process by breathing in and out more heavily than usual. Close your eyes, and to the maximum extent possible, close your mind, shutting out everything in your surroundings.

    Visualize the most peaceful scene you can develop. It could be your favorite spot at the beach, in the mountains, in a garden or at a waterfall. Anything that you find restful and serene will do. Focus on it as clearly and as completely as you can.

This process will become easier as you continue to exercise in it.

Rid yourself of all of the confusion and chaos, so you can really grasp the omniscience and omnipotence of God and rest in His peace and tranquility.

4. When you feel the effects of the peaceful condition, begin to reflect on the fact that God is the origin of creativity and that He has a new and fresh approach and answer waiting for you, tailored for your situation. Through this means you can *Know* He is right there with you and is vitally interested in your achieving the results you seek. The peace and tranquility is vitally important in that we sense His presence and nearness through it.

5. Concentrate for a while on your actual breathing in and out, insuring that you are away from noises and other distractions. I do not recommend that you lie down. Sit or kneel or form whatever other posture that is comfortable and relaxing to you, but not conducive to dropping off to sleep. Doing all of this will probably be difficult the first few times you try it. You may even find yourself dozing in the early stages of developing the process, but stay with it and it will become more effective.

6. Keeping your mind as clear as possible and remaining in a relaxing posture, visualize the conditions or circumstance you desire. Think and reflect on the best and most desirable situation which would make your life complete and circumstance more satisfactory.

7. Remembering that God is behind your creative genius and is willing to come to your aid, begin to speak to Him in positive ways, affirming the answers you seek in conversation. Realizing that the word "if" is very negative and defeating, eliminate it from your prayer and meditation process.

   Get the things you desire straight in your mind before you pray. When you enter into prayer, have the matter settled as to whether it is right for you or not. When coming to prayer you should be sure it's all right and practical for you.

In addition to affirming your answers, affirm your relationship and oneness with Him. Submit yourself to Him and make it known as a little child would — without reservation or doubts and in earnest — that God will fill your mind with wisdom and the appropriate answers will, either now or later, flow to you in response to your honest and fervent prayer.

Listen intently during your meditation, realizing that in order for God to communicate with you, you must not talk continually. As in any effective communication there must be listening as well as talking. Since God is dynamic, He can answer you now and later. Not every answer must be put off to the future.

Continue this process for as long as you are able and you can be assured that not only will you get answers, but you will establish a solid relationship with God. Eventually, you can continually commune with Him and He will continually provide His wisdom.

If certain answers don't come immediately, be patient and know that they will be on time. When it is time to be released from your prayer and meditation, go confidently on your way, managing your affairs carefully and positively. Know that God is with you, has heard you and will continually respond to you.

8. In due time you will receive leadings, urges ideas and hunches. These are from God in response to your meditations and prayers. These answers may come in the midst of your daily routines, on your way to and from work, at lunch, or at some point in your day or night. Be certain of one thing. The answers will come.

    It is imperative that we not have a fixation on one direction or upon some traditional approach. God is not traditional and will not necessarily respond to us in traditional ways. We must be open to follow His leading, whatever direction it takes. It is also important to note how and when creative answers come to you, because this is likely to be the pattern they will follow in the future. Answers and leadings come at different times for different people. For example, they come mostly in the early hours of the morning for me. They also come at other times when I am relaxed.

    Without discounting other times, once you realize the most usual pattern of flow for you, prepare to capture the thoughts because they can slip away without your ever being able to capture them again. For example, when they tend to come while you're driving or jogging, have a recorder on hand. If they come while you're sleeping, have your pad and pencil at your bedside.

9. Finally, I urge you to maintain an attitude of thanksgiving and praise just the same as if you had received answers already. The more you practice this, the more your faith and confidence will be

Overcoming the Overwhelming 113

strengthened about the nearness and faithfulness of God and your ability to achieve what you seek.

Conversely, the greater your faith and expectancy the more readily your creative mind will harmonize with the concept of a limitless storehouse that God has established for his creation and those who diligently seek his guidance will receive it.

Although there are various forms of prayer and meditation, the significant point in all of this is that prayer establishes our communion with God. This is the system of serenity which enables us to sense His presence.

No matter what your concept of Him might be or the methodology you use to approach Him, He's there. From His dynamic and creative store of limitless possibilities, He has an answer for you and is more than willing to respond to you.

It is possible for us to design a complete mental view of ourselves, filling in all of the necessary details of the lifestyle we desire. If we accept this as present reality, and act courageously on our ideas, hunches, urges and premonitions, we soon become aware that our circumstances are generated and controlled from within us and not the other way around. This is a design feature of the human system, built into us by God and it works quite well when we follow the principles relating to prayer and meditation.

The posture you assume is not important, so long as you are relaxed and feel close to God. Similarly, the words you speak are not important, as long as they represent your earnest desires and aspirations.

The principle underlying everything I've said is simple: those who come to God in prayer must believe that

He is (exists) and that He is a rewarder of them that diligently seek Him. Without faith, however, it is impossible to do this. This biblical paraphrase says it all.

We have outlined here a complete and formal method of prayer and meditation. It implies the maintenance of communion with God along with full recognition of a strong and abiding relationship with Him.

If we wish to pray for something, we must firmly focus on that thing unceasingly. In our prayer meditation process, we affirm it as actually existing. Prayer is far more than an act of wishing or exhorting God. It is a knowing by faith. We should however, leave the methods of fulfillment and the how and the why to the God of all knowledge. He knows far more possibilities than we do. Therefore we should await His leading as to the way and reasons for fulfillment.

Let us remember that God does not withhold from us. If He did it once, He'd have to do it every time, because He is a consistent God who says I change not. He wills that we have the desires of our hearts. God is willing to fulfill the law of abundance about which Jesus spoke when He said He came that we might have life more abundantly.

We must realize that there is enough good for all of us and that God gives freely and fully to all alike. It is ours as soon as we learn to pray correctly with faith.

It is worth reiterating that prayer isn't a process for moving a sluggish, unwilling God to action, but it is a process whereby we consistently seek to understand and accept His unwavering will to respond as we seek and ask.

Chapter 8

Epilogue

Yea Though I Walk...

In the early part of this book, I promised to share with you a story which has life and death significance. I want now to share that story and to show you how the principles in this book contributed so meaningfully to life. My life.

Prior to November of 1987, all who knew me considered me to be a robust, physically fit and healthy individual who took his aerobics seriously. On November first, I began to feel sluggish and tired and generally out of sorts. Because it was so unusual for me to feel that way, I immediately contacted my physician, who in turn began to search for the problem.

After four months of searching and finding my body and its organs to be functioning well within tolerances, the final examiner, a urologist, uncovered a growth in my right kidney. Further examination revealed that this growth was a malignant tumor.

Physicians came to see me with the shocking news that

this tumor was quite large and was developing a clot along the walls of my inferior vena cava. They said it appeared that the spreading malignancy was causing the clot and it was moving up the walls of the vena cava. The final blow was that my chances for survival were slight; so slight, in fact, that they would not keep me in that hospital.

Instead, the doctors referred me to another hospital where there was a urology specialist who might be able to help me. After examination at that hospital, the prognosis was confirmed and the urology specialist indicated that I had no chance without surgery. With surgery, I might have a significantly better chance.

I consented to the surgery to have the infected parts — right kidney and a section of the vena cava where the clot was settling — removed. Following the surgery, I was told that the situation looked so bad, and that the disease had so badly affected my body and was spreading so rapidly, the doctors felt they might have killed me on the surgical table if they had tried to go through with the procedure.

For these reasons they opted to close my body and allow me "to live my last few days in relative comfort." The final prognosis was six months to one year to live. It was felt that the usual treatments for cancer would do no good, so they wouldn't burden me with the pain and discomfort they usually caused. The doctors gave me a 3% chance of survival.

The only hope expressed during the next eight months was that expressed by my wife and myself. In light of the dismal prognosis, it was very apparent that my hope was clearly in the hands of God. Because of my constant association with Him and knowing the powerful works He had wrought in my life previously, I was glad to have things in His hands.

Knowing that my work in this life was not complete

Overcoming the Overwhelming 117

and having things I wanted to do with my family, I made it known before God that I was not ready to die. I wanted to live and I wanted to live in a more excited fashion than I had ever lived before — serving others, sharing and getting the most out of each day.

Having already seen this process work in my life in so many ways, I decided to imagine my healing and life after cancer. I was a bit confused because I didn't know how cancer cells looked, nor did I know quite how to visualize healing. I went into idea generation looking for an image that I could hold to represent my healing.

After several days engaging in idea generation, I awakened one morning to an exceedingly clear image just as I opened my eyes. I saw this image of "Pac Man," a popular wide mouthed figure associated with video games in the late seventies and early eighties. "Pac Man" represented the immune cells in my body. The cancer cells appeared in my mind as little round smooth-surfaced berries moving around in my body.

Then I got the picture: "Pac Man" was to move around my body chasing these little berry-looking "cells." I could hold these pictures for several minutes. My Pac Man figure would chase around, with its wide mouth, chomping on the cancer cells. I knew the minute I received it that this was the mental image that was to deliver me.

Daily I engaged in this imagination process until the time came when I just sensed that I was better and that my body was healing. I continued to see this warfare between the immune cells and the cancer cells. At times I could actually "hear" in my imagination the cancer cells popping open as they were attacked.

After eight months of faith and imagining, I received word that a urology specialist at the Cleveland Clinic wanted to meet with me and explore possibilities for additional surgery. Reluctantly I agreed to see him. Even more reluctantly, I agreed to allow him to perform surgery again. This time he would use a heart bypass machine which would give him more time to work inside by body.

I was reluctant because I felt that my faith and imagination were working. I really didn't want to betray either by consenting to surgery. I finally consented because I wanted to see if my process was actually working. The surgery was performed rather routinely and was considered very successful.

Following the surgery, the doctors reported that their pathological studies revealed considerable necrotic cells and debris in my kidney and that the large tumor had shrunk. In addition they indicated that the clot in my vena cava had no malignancy and that it was so clear that they could find no evidence of it ever having been malignant. The prognosis for my survival and continued healthy state was given as excellent!

Today I am as active as I ever was, accomplishing more than ever and getting stronger day by day. Doctors have released me to return to normal living with no medication or restrictions. I am once again engaged in vigorous physical exercises and enjoying life to the fullest.

The second surgery confirmed for me that my imagining process for healing was working and producing results. Without that surgery, I never would have had the opportunity to see so readily the effects of my imagination. I rejoice at the splendid and exciting life I am now living.

Because of what I have learned, I felt it appropriate to write this book to share with others how they can become overcomers. I only hope that you and others might see it and apply it as a means to a full, exciting and productive life.

As we have described it, this has, for me, become an

Overcoming the Overwhelming 119

extremely effective process of achievement for the person who truly wants to live a productive and enthusiastic life. I present it to you because it has meant life to me. I hope you never have to use it for that purpose, but if you do I know it will work for you when you express an abiding faith in it and the God who designed it and stands so firmly behind it. Imagining is not my innovation; it is God's. I have merely taken the time to research it and determine how it works.

I now pass it on to you.

As a result of our discovery here and the concepts we have discussed, we should never again accept or impose limitations on our lives and their inherent possibilities. Coupled with our ability to imagine is unlimited possibility. This arrangement is fully supported by the unlimited power of God to produce what we imagine.

Our possibilities are limited only by our willingness to cling to that which is imagined and acting on the divine leadings that come as a result. This is the process for making our imaginings real.

Failure and deprivation are illusions brought on by doubt and fear and our despair about the ultimate arrival of that which we seek. Those who entertain failure and deprivation as reality will experience poverty and personal despair. The longer these are held, the larger the proportions they reach. It is imperative that joy, harmony and prosperity be held firmly until they become real, no matter what the apparent circumstances.

Perhaps one of the most challenging things to do is to imagine an objective way of overcoming a difficulty and to hold onto that concept and act as if success has already been achieved. The greatest detriment to our success is despairing or giving up.

Many contrary concepts may occur — good fortune,

unwanted results and the likes, but those who can follow their imaginings in the face of these have really reached the pinnacle of prosperous and successful living. Out of chaos and inharmonious conditions we can produce peace and prosperity.

Control your mind and teach yourself to think what is right and desirable. Create a mold for what you wish to have and to be, hold onto it, and place no limits on it. It will happen. Remember always the sobering thought that the omnipotent God is in all things and through all things. He has covenanted with us to support us and to be with us to the end of the world. So expect your dreams to be realized. So live with power and overcome that which tends to overwhelm you. And " Yea though we walk through the valley of the shadow of death" we will fear no circumstance or condition. But above all we will overcome all.

"Anything might happen to me, but nothing will defeat me."

Charles M. King